This book is a written dialogue between two friends: a man of faith and a man of science who together explore issues of faith and belief, ethics and values, life passages and life's meaning. *A Rabbi and a Doctor Walk into a Bar* entertains many thought provoking and tough questions to ponder, discuss, and answer and can be used as stimulus for critical thinking about God and science among religious study groups, as well as book clubs. In that regard, we have included questions at the end of each chapter as a catalyst for discussion.

We could all benefit from a greater ease in sharing our beliefs, even if they are not all steadfast and ironclad. We need not have all the answers, or every element of our beliefs completely figured out to begin the discussion.

In *A Rabbi and Doctor Walk Into a Bar*, a shared dialogue that is both largely autobiographical and fully vulnerable, Rabbi Mark Schiftan and Dr. Frank Boehm begin the discussion. It is an intimate one in which the reader is invited to sit and listen in, as if sitting just across the table, on a host of topics such as the belief in God, life after death, the why of evil, forgiveness, pain and suffering, and so much more.

The friendship and shared curiosity revealed in these pages invites an inevitable self-reflection on the part of the reader while ensuring they will not be alone in their exploration.

—Rabbi Laurie Rice, Congregation Micah, Nashville, TN

Two remarkably gifted men, friends of many years, reflect together on life's profound questions in light of their Jewish faith. Their honesty, wisdom, and ongoing engagement with the questions shine forth in their conversations — and we, their readers, are privileged to overhear them and learn from them. Join their conversations!

—Dr. L. Gregory Jones, President, Belmont University

Readers will enjoy being a fly on the wall listening to this conversation between two learned friends about life's most challenging questions.

—Rabbi Steve Leder, author of *The Beauty of What Remains*, and *For You When I Am Gone*

In this compelling work, we are privileged spectators as Rabbi Schiftan and Dr. Boehm engage in a wide-ranging, spirited conversation that many of us have with friends, family, even with ourselves.

Yet their words, sourced from deep perspectives gained by lifetimes devoted to medicine and faith, challenge us to consider many of our own long-held beliefs. As they cordially agree and disagree, they remind us that in working to find common ground we further refine our own truth.

In a world of accelerating conflict, their civil and reasoned approach to debating the very questions that frame our attitudes and beliefs sets a brilliant example for us all to follow.
—Dr. Jeff Balser, President of Vanderbilt University Medical Center

It has been said that the informational becomes transformational when it is relational. Rabbi Schiftan and Dr. Boehm's book, *A Rabbi and a Doctor Walk into a Bar*, is a dialogue between a man of faith and a man of science who together help us better understand the beautiful and meaningful Jewish religion.

These two men have written a book that I believe Christians should read as it imparts important information on various aspects of a Jewish way of thinking and life and allows the reader to feel a closer relation to the Jewish people.

In these days of rising antisemitism, it is crucial that we better understand each other and Schiftan and Boehm help us do just that.

—Patricia Heaton, American Actress, Philanthropist, and Social Activist

Schiftan and Boehm present an enriching and honest dialogue on enduring questions of ultimate meaning.
—Shaul Kelner, Associate Professor of Jewish Studies and Sociology, Vanderbilt University

A Rabbi and a Doctor Walk into a Bar

A SHARED DIALOGUE ON FAITH AND BELIEF

RABBI MARK SCHIFTAN

DOCTOR FRANK BOEHM

© 2025
Published in the United States by Nurturing Faith, Macon, GA.
Nurturing Faith is a book imprint of Good Faith Media (goodfaithmedia.org).
Library of Congress Cataloging-in-Publication Data is available.

ISBN: 978-1-63528-257-3

All rights reserved. Printed in the United States of America.

Scripture quotations taken from the (JPS) Holy Scriptures, according to the Masoretic Text, A New Translation, copyright 1917, 1945, 1955 by the Jewish Publication Society. Used with permission. The Jewish Publication Society of America, Philadelphia, PA.

Scripture quotations marked (NJPS) taken from the Holy Scriptures, the New Jewish Publication Society Translation, according to the Traditional Hebrew Text, copyright 1985 by the Jewish Publication Society. Used with permission. The Jewish Publication of America, Philadelphia, PA, and Jerusalem.

To Harriet,
the love of my life,
whose wise counsel,
profound patience,
guidance and grace,
have made me a better partner, father, rabbi,
and human soul.
Mark

To Julie,
my best friend, confidant, critic, and the love of my life,
whose love and devotion are a blessing
for me and our family. Each day with you is pure joy.
Frank

Rabbi Mark Schiftan, Rabbi Emeritus of The Temple in Nashville, Tennessee, served as Senior Rabbi at The Temple for 23 years. Prior to this, Rabbi Schiftan served Jewish congregations in San Francisco and San Jose, California. In each of these congregations, Rabbi Schiftan brought a revitalized and reinvigorated spirit, expanding classes, programs, spiritual innovations, and social justice initiatives. Schiftan attended San Francisco State University and the Hebrew Union College in Cincinnati. He was ordained as a Rabbi in 1987.

Now retired in his role as Rabbi at The Temple, Schiftan serves as the Jewish Student Advisor and Rabbi in Residence at Belmont University in Nashville. He also serves as Chair of the Tennessee Holocaust Education Commission. Rabbi Schiftan is married to Harriet and together they have three children Ari (Beth), Sarah Rose, and Jacob (Meredith) and two granddaughters. They reside in Nashville, Tennessee.

 Dr. Frank H. Boehm, Professor Emeritus in the Department of Obstetrics and Gynecology at Vanderbilt University Medical Center, is a nationally known pioneer in the field of Perinatal Medicine and High-Risk Pregnancy. He served as Director of the Maternal Fetal Medicine Division at Vanderbilt and Vice Chair of the Department of Obstetrics and Gynecology. Dr. Boehm also served as the chair of the Vanderbilt Medical Center Ethics Committee. The author of 250 scientific articles, Boehm also authored three lay books, *Doctors Cry, Too*; *Building Patient Trust*; and *Is Your Life Successful?*

Dr. Boehm has had numerous involvements in the Nashville Jewish community including serving as President of the Jewish Federation of Nashville and Middle Tennessee and the Jewish Foundation. Boehm is married to Julie and together they have three children, Todd (Jennifer), Tommy (Lisa) and Catherine (Eric), as well as nine grandchildren. They reside in Nashville, Tennessee, and Boca Raton, Florida.

CONTENTS

Foreword by Jon Roebuck..1

Introduction by Frank Boehm
   A Rabbi and a Doctor Walk into Berlin........................5

SECTION ONE: God and Humanity 15
   A Rabbi and a Doctor Discuss...
      Belief in God...16
      Does God Know Us?...20
      On Prayer..24
      Does God Hear Our Prayer?....................................27
      Where the Soul Resides...31
      Why Evil Exists..34
      Life after Death..39
      Are You Religious?..43
      Why Is it So Hard to Talk about God? 47
      God of the Runway..50

SECTION TWO: Living a Sacred Life...............................53
   A Rabbi and a Doctor Discuss...
      Forgiveness..54
      The Importance of Friendship 58
      Why Things Happen..63
      Love 67
      A Perfect Child...71

The Tenth Commandment 75
The Sacred Nature of Relationships 79
Pain and Suffering 83
Growing Old 87
Happiness 91

SECTION THREE: Facing Our Future Challenges with Faith 97

A Rabbi and A Doctor Discuss...

Awareness 98
Being Both 102
Closure 105
A Successful Life 109
Jew Hatred 113
Jewish Vision 117
Jewish American or American Jew 122
Healthcare: A Right or Privilege? 126
Sanctuary and Safe Harbor 131
A Messianic Age 136

Epilogue 141

FOREWORD

Imagine that you walk into a coffee shop and find a quiet corner to enjoy a few moments of good coffee and morning reflection. After several minutes idle by, two guys walk in and find a seat at a table close to you. You do not intend to eavesdrop on their conversation, but something about their dialogue draws you in, inviting you to listen with interest. These two men are talking about everything from prayer, to faith, the meaning of life, the finality of death, and even the awe and wonder of God's creation. Their thoughts are intriguing, insightful, and at times dismantling. But as you listen to their conversation, parts of your own mind awaken to a renewed sense of discovery, wonder, and reflection.

As you read this book, you get the chance to listen in to an on-going conversation between two friends, who are committed to each other, their faith, and to their sense of wonder. Together they have traveled, shared many meals, and known the joy of a deep and abiding friendship. Through their dialogue, they raise the right questions and boldly share their answers. As a reader who becomes engaged in the conversation, you may find that not all their answers are complete, or satisfying, or even fully formed. The goal, however, is not to win you over to their perspective or theological stance, but to prod you into searching deeply within your own heart and mind as they invite you to join with them in the search for meaning, for perspective, and for assurances. They are courageous enough to ask the right questions and vulnerable enough to live with the tension of the unresolved answers.

What you hold in your hand is somewhat of a pilgrim's journal. These two have lived long enough to have learned a few things, experienced both joy and heartache, and found meaning in life and in their faith tradition. The answers they provide have been forged on the anvil of experience, worship, and a healthy dose of questioning belief. I applaud their effort. It is no small thing to put pen to paper. When we do, we learn to sort out our beliefs, struggle with our own doubts, and wrestle with how to best express our thoughts. While there may be those who shy away from the tough questions of life, these two seem to revel in the exercise of stretching, asking, and wondering.

It is not just that a rabbi and a doctor walk into an imagined bar… they also walked into my life. Frank and Mark are friends of mine. We have shared many of the same conversations and pondered many of the same questions that are raised in this book. I have learned from their insights, been challenged in my own beliefs, and grown to appreciate the richness of asking good questions and living with the tension of unresolved answers. We come at life from differing perspectives and theological beliefs and have learned from each other. (I now know a little Yiddish and they know some down-home Southern expressions!) But from their careful attention to the Jewish faith, I have learned much. I stand on a much firmer foundation as a Christian, having now understood more fully the life and religious expression of Jesus and first century Judaism. It is my hope that they too have grown to better understand the motivations, values, and welcoming embrace of an authentic Christian perspective. This book will not change the world… that is not its purpose. But it will make you think and dig a little deeper into your own heart where belief, experience, and faith all converge.

So, pull up a chair and eavesdrop on the conversation. Think. Reflect. Wonder. May you discover a depth of faith yet unknown, a perspective yet unexplored, and answers not yet fully formed.

Jon R. Roebuck,
Executive Director,
the Reverend Charlie Curb Center for Faith Leadership
at Belmont University, Nashville, Tennessee

INTRODUCTION

A Rabbi and a Doctor Walk into Berlin

Several years ago, as Rabbi Mark Schiftan and I were taking one of our early morning walks, Mark mentioned that he had never been to Berlin and would love someday to visit this capital of Germany, a city with 3.6 million people and many remarkably interesting sites. I told him that this was something I was also extremely interested in doing, and so we began planning our visit to the birthplace of both my parents and Mark's father. His mother was born and raised in the neighboring German-speaking country of Austria.

Over the years, Mark and I noted that we had much in common. We were both only children raised by German-speaking parents and raised with a rich Germanic culture in our homes and lives. We spoke German well enough and while both of us had been to Germany on several occasions, neither of us had been to Berlin.

So, we began making plans to visit Berlin, a trip that both of us felt was more of a pilgrimage than merely a visit to a historic and beautiful city. For me, the trip had a feeling of coming full circle from where my parents started their journey to America. The German government had legalized citizenship for children of Jews who had immigrated or escaped Nazi Germany between the years 1933 and 1945, so having filled out all the necessary documents, I was now a German citizen. I wanted to walk the streets of Berlin with my citizenship paper in my pocket highlighting the old saying that the best revenge is living well. I found it empowering that, in 1935, Germany passed the Nuremberg laws which took my parents' German citizenship away because they were Jewish and 87 years later, I got it back.

Mark and I wanted to eat German food, drink German beer, speak German, and for at least a week, live among German people, which we did abundantly!

After months of planning, we were about as ready as we would ever be for this adventure of a lifetime, one that we knew would be an adventure that would usher forth considerable emotions. Due to my age, I felt this would most probably be my last big trip, and I was eager to complete the circle started by my parents, Ludwig and Ilse, who left Germany in August of 1938 (three months before Kristallnacht – The Night of Broken Glass). I needed this trip to complete the Boehm story, one which added twenty-four new lives resulting from the paternalistic and maternalistic DNA pool given to me from my dear parents.

This trip was not just an entertaining one or a trip that was full of seeing famous or interesting sites. It was, for both of us, a trip of feeling. Everywhere we went, we felt an inner stirring that at times was intense. The most emotional event for me was visiting the Wannsee Home and Museum, but others included the visit to the Gleis 17 train station, saying Kaddish at a small synagogue on Friday evening, walking through the Jewish Museum, and the memorial to remember the murdered Jews of the Holocaust Era.

While Mark and I have been good friends for years and shared many things in our lives, I feel our friendship has deepened to a point where it has reached the friendship of the Good, which was Aristotle's highest form of friendship. In many ways, Mark is like the younger brother I never had, and I am the older brother he never had. Our friendship and the bonding we had on this trip equaled all the wonderful things that happened to me on this adventure of a lifetime.

The experience Mark and I had in Berlin resulted in an article about our trip written by Barbara Dab, editor of the Middle Tennessee Jewish newspaper, *The Observer*. The editor gave her article the title, "A Rabbi and a Doctor Walk into Berlin." There have been jokes over the years about certain professionals walking into a bar followed by a jocular punch line creating a laugh. Rabbi Schiftan and I decided to use this joke line to begin a monthly column in *The Observer* that we have used in drafting this book and have also used the line as its title, *A Rabbi and a Doctor Walk into a Bar*.

Here is what Barbara Dab wrote in *The Observer* about the trip to Berlin.[1]

> A rabbi and a doctor, each the only child of Holocaust survivors, walking buddies, longtime friends, and a 20-year age difference between them. Each searching for signs of the life their parents were forced to leave behind in Germany more than a generation ago. Each wondering if atonement and redemption are possible. Each looking for answers to questions they had carried throughout their lives.
>
> It was against this backdrop that Rabbi Mark Schiftan and Doctor Frank Boehm, both now retired, set off on what they both say was a pilgrimage to

Berlin. "It all began with our Monday walks," says Schiftan, "I had read an article in *The Atlantic* about what the German government had done to memorialize the Holocaust, and said to Frank, 'Let's go.'"

Memorial to the Murdered Jews of Europe, the official Holocaust memorial of Germany

That article, written by Clint Smith, titled "America still cannot figure out how to memorialize the sins of our history. What can we learn from Germany," lays out a path from the liberation of Auschwitz in 1945 to the present day, unpacking the ways the German government deals with their painful history. Schiftan says he had three main goals for the trip. "First, since we both have German ancestry and both our families were forced to leave, we wanted to be there to say, 'We're still here.' Second, I wanted to see what the German government did to atone and apologize for the Holocaust. And finally, I wanted to learn what have they done to teach the lessons of the Holocaust to the next generation, and to teach the broader lesson of what happens when human beings are dehumanized."

Boehm received German citizenship last year, something he says completed a circle in his family. "In 1935 the German government took away my parents' citizenship. In 2023 I got it back." Boehm says he kept his new citizenship papers in his pocket while he was in Berlin.

Smith's article begins by describing the horrors the American soldiers met when they entered Dachau and details their reactions. A subtitle in the article says, "The first memorials to the Holocaust were the bodies in the concentration camps." But neither the article, nor Schiftan and Boehm, dwell on the most obvious examples of man's inhumanity to man. The pair visited many other sites that bear witness to what happened there.

They visited Gleis 17, fifty yards of train track from which Jews in Berlin were deported to concentration camps. Along the floor of the memorial are plaques with the date, number of Jews to board the train, the names, and the camps to which they were sent. Schiftan says he read every single name on each plaque, the last one dated 1945 with just 18 Jews deported. "I needed to pay honor to those people. You see these things and realize it was an abhorrent moment in time."

Gleis 17, fifty yards of train track from which Jews in Berlin were deported to concentration camps.

The most impactful place Schiftan and Boehm visited was Wannsee, an idyllic country home outside of Berlin along the bank of Wannsee Lake. The surroundings belie the villa's dark past. Wannsee is where, on January 20, 1942, fifteen leaders of the Nazi regime gathered to discuss and refine their ideas about implementing "the final solution," the plan to exterminate for the last time, the Jews of Eastern Europe. Boehm says the experience hit him hard. "I was surprised at my reaction. I cried the hardest there." Boehm says all copies of the original 30-page plan were burned, except for one. "Here was a country at the center of culture and science of the world. For all that to end with these fifteen individuals…" Here Boehm, still moved, is at a loss for any more words.

Wannsee, an idyllic country home outside of Berlin along the bank of Wannsee Lake

Each morning, as is Schiftan and Boehm's custom, the two met up early for coffee and a walk. They roamed the streets of Berlin, walking in the footsteps of their parents, soaking in the sights and sounds of the modern-day city, and feeling surprisingly connected to their past. They even visited a local flea market. "I felt connected to my parents," says Schiftan, who is fluent in Yiddish, "I was speaking as they would to each other." Boehm says he felt accepted. "I felt a brightness there. I felt at home." Schiftan found other unexpected comforts during his wanderings in Berlin. "Everything that was a value with which I was raised was a value there. The punctuality, the orderliness, the commitment to the best way to get things done."

During the walks around the city, they encountered yet another sign of German atonement. Embedded in the cobblestones in front of many of the houses are small metal plaques, called Stolperstein, or "stumbling stone." Each of these brass cubes are engraved with the name of the person who once lived there, their birthday, and other dates, day of deportation, date, and location of death. The stones were created in 1996 by German artist Gunter Demnig, whose father fought for Nazi Germany. Demnig continues to create and place the stones today.

Frank Boehm and Mark Schiftan at Wannsee

Boehm says the Stolpersteine are but one sign the German people are continuing to remember and learn from their past. "I feel the country is saying they're sorry in the best way." Schiftan agrees. "They excel at looking at that time in history and not only doing a full atonement, but also teaching about it to make sure it is not repeated."

There were lighter moments, too. A visit to the Berlin Symphony for a performance of, wait for it, Richard Wagner (an ardent antisemite), an irony not lost on Boehm and Schiftan. "Mark wasn't sure I'd want to go," says Boehm, "But it was an incredible experience."

A visit to the Neue Synagogue brought further satisfaction that Jewish life is thriving in Berlin's small community "There were young kids running around at the day school," says Boehm. And Schiftan even took his place on the pulpit for a moment of triumph and reflection. "I felt totally at home there," says Schiftan." Still, during Friday night services, the two stood to say Kaddish (Jewish mourner's prayer). "We wanted to say it [Kaddish] even though it was not a yahrzeit (anniversary of a death). We wanted to pay respect and remember," says Boehm.

Embedded in the cobblestones in front of many of the houses are small metal plaques, called Stolperstein, or "stumbling stone"

Mark Schiftan and Frank Boehm at Check Point Charly

Just a day after their return, Boehm and Schiftan reflect on all they saw, and what they found. Schiftan says he was struck by the comparison between the book burnings in the 1930s and what is happening in the United States today. As the two stood in front of Berlin's main university, the site where 20,000 banned books were burned in 1933, Schiftan says, "We have a long way to go in this country to deal with the fear of looking at our problematic past as opposed to looking at those lessons and seeing how we can atone so it doesn't happen again." Schiftan shares a prophetic quote from German author Heinrich Heine who said, "Wherever they burn books they will also, in the end, burn human beings."[2]

Both Schiftan and Boehm say this trip was an opportunity to not only learn but to pay homage to their parents. "I was always enamored by my father's vision and his decision to leave Germany. After he heard Hitler speak in 1932, he told my mother they had to leave," says Boehm.

Schiftan says he experienced a full range of emotions. "We saw horrific sites that made me wonder how this all could have happened. And other moments where the part of me of Germanic descent felt at home. I felt my father's presence with me." Schiftan also says there are questions that stay unanswered. "I would have loved to have asked my parents: what was it like? That sense that things were closing in. What was it like leaving your family behind? How often did you think about your brothers, your mother, and what happened to them? I think my father would have loved knowing his son came back and stood as a Jew in his homeland." Boehm says, "A rabbi and a doctor walked into Berlin and felt everything that was there."

NOTES

[1] Barbara Dab, "A Rabbi and a Doctor Walk Into Berlin…" *The Jewish Observer*, July 2023.

[2] Heinrich Heine, from his play "Almador," Holocaust Library, United States Holocaust Memorial Museum, http//ushmm.org, accessed October 30, 2024.

SECTION ONE

God and Humanity

BELIEF IN GOD

Frank: It was 1967 and I was an obstetrics and gynecology resident at Yale New Haven Hospital, and I was helping take care of a patient who was having considerable problems with her pregnancy. On one of my visits with this patient, she asked if I would pray with her and I, of course, agreed. She then paused and asked a second question. "Doctor, do you believe in God?"

I was 27 years old at the time and, quite frankly, not sure of my answer. I was raised in an observant Jewish home by parents who enjoyed and practiced their Judaism and believed in God, however, I had not formed any definitive answer to this important question.

I told my patient that I did believe in God, and we bowed our heads in prayer, but as I left the patient's room, I realized I had not been completely honest. I needed to ponder this question so the next time I was asked whether I believed in God, I could answer with complete honesty and certainty.

Mark: Frank, it is interesting that this is the story you chose to open our discussion about the concept of God and the resulting possibility of a belief in that same Master of the Universe.

It has often been said, "There are no atheists in foxholes." And while that may be true, I have also come to acknowledge that neither are there any—or many—atheists in hospital beds, nor in the hearts and minds of those who gather at their loved one's bedside.

There are moments when—despite our uncertainty—we still want very much to believe in something, perhaps

Someone, who is greater than we are, with a power more magnified than ours, and with the ability to intervene in each of our lives, or the lives of our loved ones, and to perform miracles that defy logic or any rational explanation. Even if God works *through us*, and it is the hands of doctors that cure us or save us from harm or death, are these skills any less than God-given, however we might define that gift? That, too, might be viewed as an intervention of the Divine.

So, let us begin with the question asked by your patient: "Doctor, do you believe in God?"

Frank: Over the next few months after that prayer session with my patient, I began a journey to help me find an answer. Certain scientific facts began to play a significant role in achieving that answer. It is estimated that there are two trillion galaxies in the observable universe and that a typical galaxy holds one hundred billion stars. The galaxy we live in, the Milky Way Galaxy, has four hundred billion stars and has a radius of 52,850 light years. In other words, the universe around us is, to say the least, incredibly enormous.

How could all this wonder of the universe exist without a first occurrence? It seemed reasonable to assume that whether one believed in a creator called God lighting a match to create the universe, or whether it was another occurrence, a Divine presence had to exist to cause such an enormous and magnificent universe to exist. I came to believe in a formless Divine energy that I could call God, but I also needed to understand if this God played a role in the formation of life.

Humans have long tried to explain how earth, with all its contents and living forms, came into being. Over the years two explanations have risen to popular thinking. The first is that a Divine presence created the earth and all within it over a six-day process, as told in the beginning of the first book of the Hebrew Bible. I call this the "poof theory." God said "poof" and all that is contained on earth suddenly appeared with no further explanation needed.

The second explanation for the existence of God is one that I call the "evolving theory." This explanation involves a Divinity which billions of years ago started the process of evolution whereby everything changed and to which every species of complex life from trees to grass and snails to humans owes its existence. This process of how life began is, in my way of thinking, more powerful, complicated, complex, and awesome than the "poof theory" and was the theory that began to help me understand and believe in the presence of God.

A spiritual being that could provide the building blocks and process for such an incredible event as the evolution of all living things including humankind would be consistent with the power and glory of what we call God and is therefore the essence of my belief.

Mark: Frank, I think you have laid out a beautiful beginning for our attempt to take a deep dive into the belief in and nature of God. You have done so in a way that makes sense and meaning for us, and hopefully for others, in our desire and our search to create and sustain a truly inspiring and compelling relationship with our Creator.

As has been said, "The architect of the universe didn't build a staircase leading nowhere."[1] To glance in awe of the universe, the complexity of the galaxies and their stars and their planets, the cycle of each day and the order of every season…is truly breathtaking, extraordinary, and beyond our comprehension to fully grasp and understand.

As a wise rabbi once said, "God performs miracles every day. But man takes his little hand, covers his tiny eyes, and often sees none of them."[2]

For me, this enormous creative force is one of the ways I see God and affirm God's existence.

Question for Discussion and Reflection: Do you believe in God? If yes, why and if not, why?

NOTES

[1] Earl Nightingale, "The Strangest Secret," Google search AI, https://www.youtube.com/watch?v=IeaBfM3TdHQ, accessed October 30, 2024.

[2] Baal Shem Tov, *Likrat Shabbat*, ed. Rabbi Jonathan D. Levine (Bridgeport, CT: The Prayer Book Press, Media Judaica, 1981, Expanded Edition), pg 49.

DOES GOD KNOW US?

Mark: There is a Jewish blessing which directly acknowledges a close relationship between God and every single human soul: *Blessed are You, God of the universe, the Knower of all secrets.*

This short but substantive prayer suggests the belief among many that the Master of the Universe knows each of us on an intimate level, knowing our thoughts and our impulses, our strengths and our weaknesses, our hopes and our dreams, our transgressions, misgivings, and mistakes. To acknowledge that we really believe in a God that is the Knower of All Secrets, to believe that there is a God who can know even those things that no one else knows about us, who can recognize the fears we hold and hide within us, who has access to our doubts, our longings, our misgivings and regrets, who can see things that no one else can see within our hearts, our minds, and our souls…can that really be true?

Frank, as both a scientist and a man of faith, what do you think of this: Does God know us? Does it matter? And if God knows us, what can we, in turn, know about God?

Frank: Mark, you mention that God knows us on an incredibly intimate level. To understand this concept as you so beautifully described it, I need once again to turn to science.

There are approximately thirty-six trillion cells in the human adult with eighty-six billion of these cells found in the brain. Each cell in our body holds a nucleus which is made up of forty-six strands of chromosomes (twenty-three from our mother and twenty-three from our father) that carry long pieces of DNA. DNA is the material that contains genes and is the building blocks of the human body. These forty-six chromosomes have approximately 20,0000 genes making up a small amount of the entire genetic material. The remaining genetic material found among three billion base pairs aids in directing the body in an enormous variety of ways.

More than likely this genetic material contained in each brain cell aids in directing our personality, interests, likes, dislikes, mood behavior, feelings, choices, mental stability, intelligent and emotional quotient, and an enormous number of countless other aspects of our being. These brain cells, called neurons, are the computer of our body and function in an enormous number of ways to help keep us alive and functioning.

When we feel love, empathy, pain, anger, sadness, happiness, depression, jealousy, or a host of other feelings, they are produced by the interacting cells in our brain and are the result of the DNA that we obtained from our parents and all their ancestors before them. Those feelings are the result of the DNA contained in our neurons and direct so much of how we feel and what we do. I came to believe that the God I believe in is embedded in my DNA since it was this God who created me through the incredible and complex process of evolution. God's "voice and hands" direct me through the DNA God created. The God I believe in is within my human form helping direct me on a path of goodness and righteousness, speaking to me through a "Still Small Voice" (1 Kings 19:12). Mark, what do you think of this explanation?

Mark: Frank, you have offered a brilliant approach that offers a rational, logical, and scientific possibility that God knows everything about us and even speaks to us through the intricacies of the human body.

Let me offer a different, if perhaps less scientific yet more religious, more spiritual response. When I contemplate the majesty and order of the universe, the rhythms of the seasons and the years, the complex and complicated ways in which the human body is constructed and continues to exist and evolve, it is certainly possible, I believe, for the Creator of the universe, to know us in some way or another.

I am humble enough to acknowledge *the possibility* that God knows us, especially given the fact that our earliest biblical narratives describe each of us as created in the Divine Image. What a noble concept! A part of that creative force that gives and sustains life has been implanted within every human soul. If I couple that notion with the prophetic writings that further describe the "Still Small Voice" within us, we can contemplate the ways in which God offers us a moral compass, accessible to all who seek to use it.

It is possible, of course, that both of us are wrong since there is no real proof of any of this. And that may be so. But unlike others who believe that one's faith needs to be sure and ironclad, I am comfortable living in the realm of "what if?" What if it is possible, based on your scientific and my spiritual approach, that God could know us, speak to us, enter dialogue with us, as an internal part of us and our lives? Wouldn't even that possibility inspire us to better ourselves, to reflect the best within us, as a reflection of that Divine image, as an echo of that "Still Small Voice?"

That is the pathway to a richer and more fulfilling life: a life infused with both a greater meaning and with a more sacred purpose. Who would not want that kind of existence? Who would not want that way to add greater worth and meaning to our days?

Question for Discussion and Reflection: Does the God you believe in interact in your life? If so, how?

ON PRAYER

Frank: As a young child, my mother, of blessed memory, had me recite a prayer in German each night before I climbed into bed. Translated into English, the prayer said, "In God's name, I lay myself down to sleep and hope to reawaken happy and healthy." As I grew older and ceased to recite this prayer, I began to question the value and essence of prayer, yet over the years have concluded that prayer is a vital aspect of a spiritual and meaningful life. As a learned rabbi, my question to you is this: can we speak to God through the process of prayer and does God hear us?

Mark: The Siddur (the traditional Jewish prayer book) is the anthology of the Jewish people, a collection of the hopes and dreams, the longings, and aspirations of a myriad of prayers over two thousand years. Every single one of those prayers, whether petitionary in tone, or whether conveyed as an expression of gratitude, is an attempt to communicate with our Creator.

The touching memory you shared about the bedtime prayer taught to you by your mother reflects the daily prayers many are taught as children, either when we lie down or when we awaken. We are encouraged to engage in conversation with our Creator on a sustained and regular basis, just as more observant Jews will recite prayers three times a day as a community gathered in the synagogue. Most faiths embrace both rituals, both personal as well as communal prayerful attempts to speak to God.

Somehow as we grow towards maturity, many of us let these rituals fall by the wayside. We feel as though such attempts at prayer are no longer necessary in our lives. We feel as though the words no longer bear meaning or relevance. Or we no longer believe in the efficacy of prayer. We grow increasingly uncertain as to whether God hears our prayers, or responds to them, or whether there really is a God at all.

Prayer still has currency; it still has worth and value. Sometimes we need a recalibration to remind ourselves of the importance of humility and the related sense of gratitude. In this way, our prayers are heard. If it is possible that God created us, as well as the world around us, then I suppose it is equally possible that God could listen to our supplications and our expressions of gratitude.

Does it matter? Even if that turns out not to be true, then certainly we hear our prayers, as does the Divine image within us. When we gather as a community of worshipers, we hear the combined prayers of a people who have honed those words over thousands of years. That, I believe, has value, too. Together, our voices echo the sacred sounds that have attempted to reach our Creator for centuries. In that we take enormous comfort, whether God listens to those sentiments, or not. We hear, we listen, and sometimes that can be enough.

Frank: I agree with you that God hears our prayers. However, if I believe that God is in my DNA, then God lives within me, and I am responsible for my actions. For me, prayer is a process that leads me to turn inward and examine what I am looking for or need to understand. Praying to the God within me, listening to God's "Still Small Voice" helps me answer the questions I need answered to calm my restless soul. Our

Reform Judaism prayer book supports this concept: "Prayer may not bring water to parched fields nor mend a broken bridge nor rebuild a ruined city. But prayer can water an arid soul, mend a broken heart, rebuild a weakened will."[1]

I use prayer to examine the God within me to help guide me through issues that cause me emotional pain. There are other times when I use prayer to meditate on the beauty and wonder of life, as well as to find an inner peaceful moment of self-reflection. I do not use prayer to ask an outside source for something I wish to happen or thank an outside source for what has already happened. I use prayer to quietly examine the spiritual feelings within me and allow those feelings to dictate my course.

For me prayer can happen anywhere, especially where the beauty of nature exists. However, it is when I sit in my temple, reciting the mantra of ancient words that I learned as a young child, that prayer seems to flow more easily and with more reflection and intensity.

Question for Discussion and Reflection: When you pray, to whom do you pray?

NOTE

[1] Rabbi Abraham Joshua Heschel (adapted), Mishkan Tefillah: *A Reform Siddur*, Rabbi Elyse Frishman (ed.), CCAR Press: New York, 47.

DOES GOD HEAR OUR PRAYER?

Mark: In many Reform synagogues, like mine, a prayer for healing has been reintroduced in recent years. Though always a part of traditional Jewish worship, it was abandoned by Reform Jews because it was felt to be a theological bridge too far for many to cross: it was one thing to assemble as a congregation to engage in prayer; it was another thing, entirely, to ask God to actually intervene in our lives in a vivid, dramatic fashion, answering our prayers for healing with a miraculous cure or intervention, whether for us or for our loved ones.

But over these past few years, even as we have seen the miracles of modern medicine, we have also witnessed the limitations in the reach of that medical science, so we have come to look for additional assistance from a Higher Power. We, who are rational human beings in most moments, become more religious human souls, searching, pleading for Divine answers or even Divine intervention, when confronted with something we cannot control.

In most Jewish worship services today, the Misheberach, the prayer for healing, is one of the most fervent prayers that is uttered. It is also the one that was abandoned years ago, the words banished from the Reform Jewish prayer book. Now it has not only been brought back but has become the most meaningful part of the entire service. Names of the infirm are often uttered aloud before the prayer begins, and then God is asked to intervene; to heal, to strengthen, console and comfort, to provide courage and consolation.

So, does God answer these prayers? Do those who offer these prayers expect an answer? How would we know for sure? And what if those prayers go unanswered? What then?

Here is what I believe: the God beyond us, the God of the heavens, intervenes and answers, or that God does not. What I do believe is that it is certainly possible. Why does God respond to some prayers and not to others? That I do not know or understand, nor do I need to pretend to know the answer to that mystery. That is beyond my range of knowledge or comprehension. And that, for me, is okay.

What I also believe is this: the God within each of us, the Divine Image we all share, does respond with answers on a regular and consistent basis. That God inspires us with strength and courage. That God summons our abilities to offer comfort, compassion, and consolation. That God grants the intellectual and human gifts that allows physicians and nurses to cure, to remedy, and to heal. That God answers our prayers often. Frank, how does this answer square with your thoughts and beliefs?

Frank: Mark, I agree with you on one aspect of your answer about prayer but disagree on another. You state God may or may not answer our prayers! Which one is it? I agree with your statement that God offers comfort and inspires us with strength and courage. I agree with you that God summons our abilities to offer compassion, and consolation.

I do not believe God answer's prayers with direct intervention. However, praying to God gives you the needed strength and courage to manage the difficulties that life brings and can help bring peace to a troubled soul and calm to an anxious heart. Prayer does not cure cancer or heart disease, or any other requested miracle. That voice of God merely guides us, helps us understand how to deal with adversity, and gives us the strength to get through the tough times.

So, Mark, we agree and disagree on this issue of prayer. That is what we Jews do.

Mark: Frank, as a physician, you certainly know about the human heart, that it can harden over time. When we read the Exodus story, Pharaoh suffered from the same affliction, though perhaps his was more figurative than literal. Just the same, we know that a hardened heart can have severe negative implications and effects on those who suffer from such a condition.

Well, what if I told you that I believe that one of the ways I have seen God answer prayers is through God's intervention to soften our hearts, even when they have been hurt, or broken, and make them open their same constricted heart muscles, once again. Not necessarily in a physical sense, but rather, in a spiritual one allowing hope, promise, and uplift to make their hearts soften and operate at full function yet again. Frank, think about the people you know and see if this concept resonates with you and holds true.

A friend is discouraged after a failed marriage or two and swears never to get married again. But God directs him to a partner of his dreams and his heart is softened and opened once again. Or another friend, a widow, her heart broken and closed, finds her way, unexpectedly, to open her heart to love once again, her heart softened, her crushed spirit made whole again.

Or a parent has a wayward child, their heart embittered and hardened. They cannot even fathom the choices their child has made. Yet something—or Someone— softens that parent's heart with an extraordinary sense of compassion, opening it to find a way back to their child.

Or a child is born with a debilitating condition, making a parent or grandparent wonder about their ability to fully love and embrace that child. What eases that weight on their heart, what allows it both to soften as well as to strengthen its ability to love that child in new ways, in ways beyond measure?

In this way, and others, I believe it is possible that God may answer our prayers and heal our wounded hearts.

Frank: Mark, you make a wonderful argument for the prayer I believe in. In all your examples of a wounded heart that is healed by prayer, prayer allowed the person to turn inward and listen to that "Still Small Voice" that helped heal the broken or misguided spirit. It was the God within each of these individuals that helped that person move forward with their life. No external God heard a prayer and intervened. It was the God within that guided the path to love and acceptance. See, we agree!

Question for Discussion and Reflection: What are your expectations of prayer?

WHERE THE SOUL RESIDES

Mark: Traditional Jews awaken each morning with an initial prayer on their lips to start each day: "I give thanks unto You, O God, that, in mercy, You have restored my soul within me."

This prayer is further magnified in the liturgy of the daily morning service in the synagogue: "God, the soul you gave to me is pure. You have created it, you shaped it, and you breathed it into me, and you preserve it deep inside of me. And someday you will take it from me, restoring it to everlasting life."

This idea of a soul within each of us, pure and restored to our care each day...what is it? What does it mean to begin pure and unvarnished? And where does it go, if we believe it leaves us each night and is returned to us each new day? What does it mean when the prayer says that someday it will be taken from us and return to everlasting life?

This soul—neshama, in Hebrew— where does it exactly dwell within us, and how can we even be certain about its very existence with us?

Frank, have you considered any of these questions and pondered any answers about the human soul?

Frank: Mark, you ask so many excellent questions. I believe each of us is born with a conscience and a will and that conscience and will is God within us. This conscience is our soul. The soul is defined as the spiritual part of a human being and therefore when asked where the soul resides, I consistently answer that the soul resides in the DNA embedded in the billions of cells in our brain that is the handiwork of the God that created us.

This helped to explain why, when I did something that was not "God-like," I felt a pang of guilt or remorse. That was God speaking to me in quite vivid ways. Yet when my actions were consistent with goodness and righteousness my feelings were of pride and well-being, once again God was speaking to me through my soul, my conscience.

Where this soul goes after we die is a question that is more difficult to answer. The easiest answer for me is that our soul takes residence in those we leave behind, those we loved and those who loved us in an everlasting memory of the soul we once had. What do you think of all this?

Mark: Frank, I find your description of the soul to be fascinating and quite insightful. The rationale for the soul to be found within the brain reminds me of the ancients who believed that the mind was found within the human heart. Wherever its location, the possession of a soul is unique to human beings alone. It is the critical part of that which distinguishes us from the animal kingdom.

That critical distinction, the ability to weigh our thoughts and our actions, and whether to feel good or bad about them, that embedded conscience within us, I believe comes *from beyond us*. It is truly God given. It is the necessary building block, even the cornerstone of our ability to construct a moral life. When the prophets allude to that "Still Small Voice" within us, that is the closest we can come to understanding the concept of the human soul.

I love the concept in Jewish belief that the soul we are given at the outset of our lives is a pure one. Judaism differs here significantly from other faiths, who describe the soul as less than pure, even tarnished, in both immediate and in continuous need of repair and redemption. In our tradition, we begin our lives with a clean slate, free of any Original Sin.

I also love the idea that the ultimate ownership of the soul is not ours; it belongs to our Creator. It is lent to us, entrusted into our care and safekeeping. And to make the point, we believe the soul is returned to us each dawn, at daybreak, as the blessing suggests. In a sense, that soul, that conscience, that moral compass, that "Still Small Voice" needs to be rediscovered and then reactivated every single day.

Finally, within Jewish tradition there is this idea of the eternity of the soul, the belief that long after our lives have ended, that soul returns somehow to its Source. Do I believe that? I do not know. But I am comforted by that thought, and I humble myself in the hope of that possibility.

Frank, I know we will discuss the afterlife in a later chapter, but I do love the idea of the soul surviving in the hearts of our loved ones. Either destination, whether returning to the Source of life, or whether entering the hearts of those most significant in our lives, is a very meaningful and comforting place for our souls to be.

Question for Discussion and Reflection: Where do you believe the soul resides? How do you define a soul?

WHY EVIL EXISTS

Frank: I am convinced that humans have free will and when that free will is abused for evil actions, those individuals either could not hear or were incapable of listening to the God within them. They are nature's genetic mutation of the conscience, and their genetic wiring lacks the necessary elements of "God-like" behavior.

How else is one to understand or explain the evil actions of humanity? How else is one to explain the Nazi Holocaust that caused the extermination of six million Jews? God did not do this. It was perpetrated by individuals who were unable to listen to the God within them. I believe that this behavior of evil will eventually evolve positively into DNA that will produce all humans to be able to hear that "Still Small Voice" and display goodness and righteousness in their actions. As the late president Ronald Reagan said, "I know in my heart that man is good, that what is right will always eventually triumph and there is purpose and worth to each and every life."[1] Humans are still evolving and someday, these words of Ronald Reagan will come true.

This concept of a conscience within us that strives for goodness in life is not a new one. Neuroscientists have explained that humans experience pain when we see pain in others, and we call this trait empathy. According to these neuroscientists, humans are moral animals, and it is this morality within us that is the God that lives within us. The famous German theologian Dietrich Bonhoeffer emphasized this point. "God has given everyone a conscience and with this conscience he or she is God."[2]

I am aware that my explanation of why evil exists is not an easy one to accept. What is your opinion on this?

Mark: Evil is as old as the Bible itself; it is as ancient as the earliest recorded stories of the creation of humankind. Despite God declaring that God's creation was "very good," the introduction of evil and the declension of its consequences follows immediately after the creation of the first human beings.

Cain murders Abel in the heat of anger, Noah and his family are the only ones saved in the face of a morally bankrupt society, and Abraham argues with God, unsuccessfully, to save the cities of Sodom and Gomorrah if at least ten righteous souls in the entire area can be found, which they are not.

According to Jewish tradition, every one of us is created with two internal impulses: one that encourages us to *be* good, to *do* good; and the other one, its opposite, the one that creates and sustains the evil inclination within us. The challenge of being given free will is to hopefully often, if not necessarily always, choose the good impulse over the evil one.

Why is there evil in this world? Why was it introduced? Why does it continue to exist, and even at times, to thrive? I wish I knew. I truly wish I could understand why God would allow it to enter our world and continue to inflict the damage it causes to so many. Evil acts, large or small, cause immeasurable pain and suffering, both to individuals and to entire groups and classes of humanity.

Rabbi Harold Kushner (of blessed memory) offered a radical yet compelling theology that offered comfort to millions. He proffered the notion that God *does not* or *cannot* control everything. Therefore, evil exists right alongside goodness.[3]

This is what I believe: Religion, done right, is neither judgmental, nor repressive nor punitive. Religion, done right, makes us better human beings. It harnesses our goodness as the best counterweight to the evil that exists around us, and even, at times, within us. Religion, done right, sustains the Divine flame within each of us, in the way a single flame can help keep darkness at bay. It can make us more kind, more caring, more sensitive human beings who respond as God's partners fight and overcome evil by seeking to alleviate pain and suffering, and by offering solace and sanctuary to the wounded souls who reside among us.

Eventually, it is this overwhelming collaborative goodness which can inevitably prevail over evil. As Dr. Martin Luther King offered: "The arc of the universe is long, but it inevitably bends towards justice."[4] Frank, does this resonate with you?

Frank: Mark, I do not completely agree, but there is an element of faith and belief that overlaps. You believe that each of us is born with two internal impulses, one that encourages us to be good and to do good and the other that is the exact opposite. I, on the other hand, believe that while most of us are born with the will to do good, there are others who have moral mutations who have difficulty in hearing the "Still Small Voice" that urges us to do and act good.

Your theory allows you to believe that religion plays an influential role in helping us to act in a moral manner, while my theory is that religion plays a much less significant role.

The individual who lacks the ability of the God within to be heard, may be influenced to do good and act good by a process of nurturing using the principle of epigenetics. That process is defined as a stable change of cell function induced by nurturing, which happens without change to the DNA sequence. In other words, evil DNA can be overridden by nurturing aspects of several factors, including religion.

Not everything, when it comes to genetics, can be considered black or white. There are many influences on behavior, but it seems reasonable to assume that nature makes up approximately 80% of who we are, and nurture makes up the remaining 20%, and that this 20% can be significantly influenced and mollified by religion.

Mark, what is your reaction to all of this?

Mark: Frank, I agree with what you believe about the role of nurture over nature, in the way that perhaps the nurturing of the good can override the inclination to do harm. While this may not hold true for some who are possessed by incorrigible evil or heinousness, it can certainly hold true for many others. Truthfully, even those who normally strive to lead good lives require occasional reminders to guard against apathy or indifference.

The Passover Seder rituals recall our suffering and forced servitude under Egyptian bondage. Those rituals *could* focus our thoughts on our own trauma, causing us to embitter our hearts, and to therefore refrain from our caring and concern for others. There is a choice we then must make: our painful past can either make us bitter, or better.

Repeatedly, religion helps us choose to be better, to harness our suffering, to make us more empathetic to others in distress, and to let the good impulse within us prevail. That is how God works through us to counter the evil around us and within us, wherever it may exist.

Question for Discussion and Reflection: Why do you believe evil exists?

NOTES

[1] Bret Baier with Catherine Whitney, *Three Days in Moscow: Ronald Reagan and the Fall of the Soviet Empire*, (Nashville: Harper-Collins, 2018), 107.

[2] Eric Metaxas, *Bonhoeffer: Pastor, Martyr, Prophet, Spy*, (Nashville: Thomas Nelson Publishing, 2011), 92.

[3] Rabbi Harold Kushner, *When Bad Things Happen to Good People* (New York: Schocken Books, 1989, 2nd edition), 134.

[4] Martin Luther King, "Our God Is Marching On" speech delivered on the steps of the Alabama State Capitol in Montgomery, AL, March 25, 1965.

LIFE AFTER DEATH

Mark: For all of us who live, the question we must ultimately confront concerns what happens after our death. Is there an existence beyond the grave? And if so, what is it like?

There are faith traditions that offer specific, concrete theories on the afterlife. Some describe specific locations: Heaven, for people who have lived lives of goodness; Hell, for those who did not; and a place in between, a limbo or purgatory, a waiting room of sorts for those who need a little bit more evaluation before a final decision on their ultimate destination is confirmed.

For some religions, this life is but a gateway to an eternal life, to the life that really matters. Even more, some faiths place very narrow entryways through the Gates of Heaven. To gain access to those heavenly heights, one must ascribe to a certain belief or dogma; it is either their way or the highway.

Judaism presents a unique understanding of what happens after we die. Though there are a myriad of theories that exist in Jewish tradition, including rabbinic texts that describe various views of heaven, resurrection (and even other more obscure concepts and beliefs), Judaism is comfortable with the idea that none of us knows, for sure, what happens after we die, largely because no one has ever come back to tell us about what happens when our lives have ended.

Admittedly, for some, this is of little comfort because it suggests the sobering possibility that *this* life is the *only* life we will ever have. Perhaps this is why Reform Judaism encourages us to make our lives a blessing, both to the God who created us and to those with whom we share this world of ours. It is why whenever we refer to someone who has passed away, we say "May his or her memory be remembered as a blessing." I am comforted by this assumption that this life is all we have, for sure, and that our time is therefore even more precious and more meaningful, because this is it.

When someone dies in Jewish tradition, we recite the Kaddish prayer over their memory. The prayer does not speak of death, but rather of life and of our gratitude for the gift of the life of our loved one, given to us by the God who created it. It is an affirmation of the worth of the life of the one we have lost, yet still love.

The everlasting life I believe in is something I describe as "The Heaven of the Human Heart." That is, we live on in the hearts and minds of those who survive us and come after us, in memories we leave behind for our loved ones to cherish, in the stories they recall and retell about us, and through the things we taught them either by word or by deed. That is our legacy and our eternity. And for me, that is good enough. In fact, it is more than enough. And it is an afterlife in which I can believe.

Frank, what is your view of the life after death?

Frank: On this subject, Mark, we are in total agreement. I am comforted by the fact that I strongly believe that my life on earth is the only life I will ever know, and that when I die, I will spend eternity in a sleep without dreams. I remember nothing about the world before I was born, and I will know nothing about the world after I die. I do not have to worry about heaven or hell. Those two "places" are found right here on earth during my lifetime.

As first year medical students, our class of fifty-two students was divided into groups of four and assigned a cadaver to dissect and study to understand the very foundational and anatomical aspects of the human body. I memorized every part of the human body and could show our anatomy professor where each structure was found, but I was also able to begin a journey of a spiritual understanding of the human body.

The most significant aspects of my spiritual education while dissecting the human anatomy was the simple fact that our cadaver made me realize that when we die our physical life was over, and if there was life after death, it did not involve the physical body. The next question needing an answer was reduced to; if there is life after death, how exactly is that defined?

During that first semester in medical school, I came to believe that life after death consisted primarily of the memories and deeds that my life shared and created and that I would eventually leave those deeds and memories to my loved ones and friends in an everlasting fashion.

It has been said that when we die, we die twice. First, when we take our last breath and then again when the last person who remembers us dies. But during those early medical school years it seemed to me that there needed to be more extension to this belief in life after death and it should not end merely when the last person who remembers us dies.

I came to believe that the words of wisdom I spoke during my lifetime and the values I lived by would all be passed, not merely to those I loved and knew but that these same individuals would then in turn pass some aspect of my life's wisdom and deeds from generation to generation, initially in quite vivid memory and then later only as an echo of who I was in much more subtle and difficult ways to trace or understand.

It seemed to me that I am who I am because my father and mother left me with not only genetic traits and characteristics but also with a moral and ethical code of behavior called spiritual DNA. They in turn received their spiritual DNA from their parents and friends who received theirs in similar fashion. I am in so many ways the result of relatives and others who passed down to me their collective attributes over the generations in quite subtle ways and would help explain a doctrine of living long after we are no longer alive or remembered by anyone alive. That belief was quite comforting to me as a young man of only twenty-five years and it is what I still believe to this day, sixty years later.

Mark: We can also be remembered by people with whom we share a sort of communal spiritual DNA. In the synagogue, we read the names each week of those who died at that season in years past. In my congregation, those names extend back more than one hundred and fifty years. As I grow older, the recitation of those names has taken on an even greater meaning to me, perhaps because I am deeply comforted by the thought that within that same sacred space, my name will be added to that list, to be recited as well. Those gathered there and then, will recite the Kaddish prayer, over me, affirming my time on earth, even many years after I am gone.

Question for Discussion and Reflection: What happens to us after we die?

ARE YOU RELIGIOUS?

Mark: People are often uncomfortable responding to questions of faith and belief. This is even more so the case when they are asked to evaluate themselves regarding their own personal religious practice. Often, they will describe themselves as "spiritual, but not necessarily religious" in terms of their adherence to certain rituals or as measured by their church or synagogue affiliation or attendance.

There are, however, those who describe themselves as "believers." For them, their attachment to their faith is directly connected to their obedience to a set of standards, rules of ritual practice, and regular and active participation in a religious community and House of Worship.

Others bristle at this definition of religiosity; it is neither a compelling nor a comfortable description of how they view themselves and their connection to their faith traditions.

I have found that many, even most, non-traditional Jews find it uncomfortable to describe themselves as religious. There is something about the term that conjures up negative images or disturbing stereotypes in their minds. Somehow, many of us have come to see defining ourselves as religious creates a negative, limited, or narrow view of how we wish to see ourselves and define ourselves.

Frank, what is your take on this?

Frank: I have often pondered the question of what constitutes a religious person but have never felt satisfied with the responses I have heard others give when asked this very personal question. Often the response is, "I am Jewish and a member of our Temple, but I really do not believe I am a religious person." Other common responses include, "I am more of a spiritual person than a religious one" or "I am more a secular Jew than a religious one." So, the big question is, what defines a religious person?

I believe a person is religious when one listens to the "Still Small Voice" within each of us and is guided in the direction of being a good and thoughtful person who believes in equal justice, who is empathetic, peaceful, and loving when dealing with others. That can all be summarized by what is quoted in Leviticus, "Thou shalt love thy neighbor as thyself" (Leviticus 19: 9–18). Following the Golden Rule is all one really needs to do to be a religious person.

In his book on Abraham Lincoln titled, *And There Was Light*, historical writer Jon Meacham writes, "To Lincoln, God whispered His will through conscience calling humankind to live in accord with the laws of love."[1] That was Lincoln's description of religion. Deed was more important to him than creed.

In 1930, Rabbi Julius Mark of the Vine Street Temple in Nashville, gave a talk to a group of assembled Jews and Christians and stated, "Whether a man belongs to a Synagogue or Church or Mosque or no church at all, he needn't worry about his soul, provided he lives a righteous life on earth and if he belonged to every church in the world and went to one every day of his life and prayed with all his being, I shouldn't give a rap for his soul if at the same time he was dishonorable, unjust, unkind, a cheat, and a liar or a hypocrite."[2] Others throughout history have said quite the same thing.

The "Still Small Voice" that lives in all of us is what should help us know how to act in this world. It is the voice of God speaking to us. Being religious is to listen to that voice and treat our fellow human beings with kindness, fairness, and understanding. It is not how often we attend religious services or practice the laws and rules of our religion. It is the deed and not the creed that makes one a religious person.

Mark: Would it not be wonderful if everyone could harness the "Still Small Voice" all on their own, at any time they chose to do so, always at the right time, place, and manner? We could lock the doors to every church, mosque, and synagogue, permanently cancel every worship service and put each building up for sale, because there would no longer be any use for them. People could sustain their religious faith and behavior all on their own.

I believe that religious rituals and traditions, housed in places of worship, are the needles on the moral compasses of our lives. They are the bedrock of those deeds you define as being valued over creed, though they also often articulate those creeds quite well as guideposts to emulate. These sacred venues, as well as the communities they create, are there to foster, sustain, nurture, and remind us of the obligations we have to those beyond our *own* selves and our *own* needs. Those rituals within those sacred spaces sanctify and magnify the most meaningful moments in our lives. They also elevate our lives by reminding us of the higher purpose of our lives as carriers of the Divine Image within us.

Rabbi Hillel taught: "If I am not for myself, then who will be for me? But if I am only for myself, then who am I? And if not now, then when?"[3] There is a reason Jews must form a minyan, a quorum, to say certain prayers, including the Kaddish prayer in memory and in honor of the deceased. We need that quorum because we cannot exist alone in sustaining a religious tradition: in the end, either we exist within a community of faith, or our religion will cease to exist.

To be Jewish solely in one's heart, Judaism teaches us, is insufficient. Judaism—as with other faiths—is kept alive by actions that strengthen the community that cherishes its faith together. The deed of commitment to one's people surpasses the creed of a single individual's expression of belief.

In the end, while we may not choose to follow every commandment or practice every ritual, we are also encouraged not to stand alone. When we enter the synagogue, we listen to the echoes of our ancestor's prayers, we engage in a worship service that is at once familiar and comforting to them as it is to us, and by our sheer presence, we strengthen our community of faith, even as it strengthens us.

If that does not remind us how to be good, if that does not challenge us to be even better people, I do not know what does. You do not need religion to be a good person, but it cannot hurt us in our attempts to be one.

Question for Discussion and Reflection: How would you define being religious?

NOTES

[1] Jon Meacham, *And There Was Light*, (New York: Random House, 2022), 16.

[2] Rabbi Julius Mark, remarks to Ecumenical Meeting, Nashville, TN, 1930.

[3] Hillel quote: Mishnah, Pirke Avot, *Sayings of the Ancestors*, 1:14.

WHY IS IT SO HARD TO TALK ABOUT GOD?

Mark: Jews are the first people to believe in monotheism, yet we are so hard pressed to share our theological beliefs with others, even with those whose opinions we value and whose confidences we trust. We treat our beliefs as a private matter in our daily lives and yet we engage in offering public prayer throughout our lifetimes. We grow uncomfortable with starting the conversation, growing increasingly more uncomfortable when others open the discussion as well.

We could all benefit from a greater ease in sharing our beliefs, even if they are not all steadfast and ironclad. We need not have all the answers, or every element of our beliefs completely figured out to begin the discussion.

Are you a religious skeptic? To be perfectly honest, I am. I am a man of faith who regularly struggles with my belief in God. I am a member of the clergy who believes in the possibility of a Higher Power but who often doubts and questions that very existence of God. I am a rabbi who finds wisdom in the name by which my people define itself: "Yisrael"—or Israel—the Hebrew term for "One who wrestles with God."

I take great comfort in that wrestling, that questioning, that search for the Source of all creation. I often question what God asks of us, and dare I say, what we might demand of God in return. There is a holiness in wrestling for those answers, both those we seek and those we find, as well as those that elude our grasp or our ability to fully understand or comprehend.

For some religious traditions, such questioning of one's faith or one's belief in God is blasphemous, but for my people, and for me, it is nothing short of sacred.

Let me invite you to consider this challenge: to doubt and to ponder as to whether there is a God, or not, is a sacred enterprise, especially if we allow ourselves to believe that *even the potential existence of the Divine presence in our lives can suffice.* It can be enough for us to describe ourselves as religious, or as spiritual, each of us engaged in trying to find our way to make a meaningful life, a holy existence, each of our journeys a search for meaning, for purpose, and for seeking a relationship with our Creator and the Source of our lives.

Are you an agnostic, open to the possibility of the existence of a God, but far from certain without sufficient or concrete evidence of His existence? So am I.

For me, that mystery is what makes the journey of exploring the possibilities of faith and belief so exciting, so open to possibility and so inviting to discussion among us. Frank, what about you? Why do you think so many people are so hesitant to openly discuss and share our views about God?

Frank: Mark, you have said what so many believe, in such a beautiful and meaningful way and you have clearly uttered the words that have filled my heart since I was a young man. Ever since a patient asked, when I was only twenty-seven years old, if I believed in God, I have like Jacob, wrestled with finding an answer. While I came to my belief in God in a scientific manner, I, nonetheless, still question if my belief is firm and true.

That is what Jews do and that is what we are supposed to do. To be certain about something so important is to remove humility from our soul and that is something that the God I believe in would not ask of me. I am not afraid of talking to others about the uncertainties of my belief in God.

Mark: Frank, I appreciate what you just wrote as I believe that faith requires the profound act of humbling yourself, acknowledging that you are neither the center of the universe nor its Master. It requires the ability to consider the possibility that there is a Source or Force of creation that is higher and greater than you. Faith offers the comfort of realizing that we neither have all the answers nor are we even entitled to know all the answers to any of the questions, ponderings and doubts we have about this gift we call Life. Our wrestling with God is our pathway towards crafting a more sacred and spiritually honest life.

Question for Discussion and Reflection: Are you a religious skeptic? If so, why?

GOD OF THE RUNWAY

Mark: When I was preparing for my rabbinic school interview, one of the questions I felt I would certainly be asked about was my belief in God and the specific nature of that belief. I was prepared to be challenged by my belief, as well as to offer a window into the depth and sincerity of that belief.

But the question never came up! How could that be? How could that query and its adequate response not be among the most critical of questions for determining my competency and readiness for a proper rabbinic seminary education?

To further the point, I was never asked any related questions about my belief in God by any of the various search committee interviews I sat through during my thirty-six years in the congregational rabbinate. How could this be?

Nonetheless, I spent much of my career feeling as though I always needed to have one concise, cogent, and consistent answer, whenever or wherever the question might arise.

As the years went by, I realized that the idea of having just one answer, or of one simple, unwavering response, was no longer satisfactory to me, nor could it be, after all I had learned and all I had witnessed as a rabbi, nor would it be an honest answer for my congregants. I had developed many concepts of God, and as I grew more comfortable expressing a multiplicity of answers and beliefs, I felt it might open the possibilities of belief for others, as well.

Here's what I believe: I believe in the God that exists *within* each of us; I believe in the God that is found in the relationships *between* us; I believe in the God that *formed* and *sustains* the world around us; and, at times, I even believe in the God *above* us, the anthropomorphic God we acknowledge the most through prayer. I call that version of God, the God of the airplane runway.

Here is why: There are times in each of our lives when rational explanations for things cease to work for us. For me, one of those times is when I am seated on an airplane waiting for takeoff at the edge of the airplane runway. At those moments, as I contemplate the unbelievable miracle of flight, along with what it means to be propelled through the sky in a heavy metal tube, I believe in and pray to a very anthropomorphic type of Deity, whom I call the God of the airplane runway. I take comfort in the image of the arms of my Creator, which lifts that plane and, defying the laws of gravity, carries it across miles upon miles on thin air, and then sets it down, ever so gently, once again, often halfway across the world. To that God, I offer the same prayer before every takeoff, taking great comfort in the belief and hope that my God of the airplane runway will listen, keeping the plane aloft and keeping me (and my fellow passengers) safe.

Frank, does anything about this make sense to you or resonate with you?

Frank: Yes, Mark, and it is what I believe, as well. Jews often recite the Shema, (the central Jewish prayer that affirms God's oneness and incomparability) before they die, including the Jewish martyrs who, throughout the ages made it their final profession of faith before being put to death. My parents told me when I was young that the Shema was what they believed to be the last words a dying Jew should recite, and it is one that I have embraced. "Hear O Israel: Adonai is our God, Adonai is One. Praised be God's name whose glorious sovereignty is forever and ever," are words I have recited in Hebrew and English many times in my life. I have recited them at religious services and at times when I needed spiritual courage, such as just before I am put to sleep for a medical procedure or as you have explained so eloquently, just before the airplane I am on is about to take off. These words comfort me and allow me to feel that if something untoward happens during surgery or my trip into the air, I will have fulfilled the act as told to me by my parents. I am not sure that these words will protect me, however, I do know that they comfort me.

I am also comforted by the fact that the religious views you delve into are in so many ways the same as my scientific ones. Albert Einstein said it best, "Science without religion is lame. Religion without science is blind."[1]

Question for Discussion and Reflection: Do you offer a prayer in times of fear or stress? If you do, why?

NOTE

[1] Albert Einstein, "Science and Religion," *New York Times Magazine*, (November 9, 1930), 1–4.

SECTION TWO

Living a Sacred Life

FORGIVENESS

Frank: Mark, while on our trip to Berlin, we often spoke about issues surrounding the topic of forgiveness. I thought we should focus on this issue, and I will begin by asking: do you believe there are instances and events which we are just unable to forgive?

Mark: Frank, the whole concept of forgiveness—both our ability to offer it to others, as well as our desire to receive it in return—is both extremely complex and emotionally complicated. This is especially true for acts which are unforgivable: acts of violence, sexual abuse, neglect, and of course, heinous acts of hatred designed to terrify and terrorize other human beings. I am not sure these actions that so clearly dehumanize others are forgivable under any circumstances. Certainly, it is not in our power to forgive others—like the Nazis—for the brutality brought upon our people. What are your thoughts about this, especially after our trip to Berlin?

Frank: I agree with you that there are acts which are unforgivable and the Holocaust would certainly be one of those events, but I do not believe we should continue to withhold forgiveness to Germany and all Germans living now for the crimes against our people during the time of WWII. Germany is doing all it can to admit their crimes, teaching it to all students and adults and pledging to never let such an atrocity happen again.

We saw this while visiting Holocaust museums throughout Berlin, in the busloads of students taken to various museums of horror, something our own country has not done. In contrast to Germany, we are unwilling to acknowledge the historical injustices of our own country.

Mark: Frank, I totally agree with you. Just as we cannot forgive the Nazis for what they did to desecrate and dehumanize our people, we also cannot hold the current generations of Germans responsible for the crimes that were perpetrated before them. In our own country, there is still a need to accept and acknowledge our own transgressions.

As we approach the High Holy Day season annually, we can bring this down to the more basic level of human relationships, the attempts to seek forgiveness from those we have wronged, and to offer it to others who may have offended us. Of course, these are among the most difficult tasks to undertake as human beings because they incur the risks of vulnerability and complete contrition. Still, these efforts can set our minds free, release our souls from the burdens we carry, and allow us to make peace with ourselves, our neighbors, and even with our Creator.

Frank: Mark, when I consider forgiveness, I am most interested in the important principles surrounding the process of forgiveness. The three basic principles of asking for forgiveness are:

1. Recognizing the wrong you did.
2. Recognizing the negative impact of what you did.
3. Taking ownership of, and asking forgiveness for, both the first and second of these principles.

Conversely, the person wronged must feel that the person asking for forgiveness is truly repentant and that when you state, "Yes, I forgive you," you are also agreeing to another three principles which are:

1. Not to ever bring it up again.
2. Not to ever bring it up to anyone else.
3. Not to ever bring it up to yourself as well.

Mark: You have it exactly right, Frank. I would only add one thing to your list, for the one seeking forgiveness: a pledge to *never, ever* commit the same offense again, recognizing and fully understanding the harm inflicted on the one to whom an apology is due.

This is the beauty of our Jewish tradition. Once each year, we take a measure of our time on earth, and of our conduct towards others. And before we dare seek forgiveness from God, our tradition requires that we first make peace with our neighbors and try to reconcile with one another.

Frank: Mark, there is another principle of forgiveness we also need to mention—that is to be able to forgive oneself. This is truly a difficult thing to do as you are both the offender and the one being offended. Here is where guilt plays a key role, as guilt is an incredibly destructive emotion that desperately needs our personal forgiveness. It is under these circumstances that prayer can be of immense help and the Jewish High Holy Days is an opportune time to find a way to forgive oneself through reflection and prayer.

Mark: Frank, I love this concept of forgiving oneself, so long as it does not release us from the need to continue to seek forgiveness from others. I believe that we all harbor regrets that can burden our thoughts and weigh heavily upon our hearts. We all have deeds we wish we could undo, or words that we could take back that should never have escaped from our lips. Even worse, there are actions taken against those we love, including those who no longer live. Perhaps it was our inaction or inattentiveness for which we now have remorse.

By acknowledging and accepting our shortcomings, our failures, and our regrets, our High Holy Days can help us to heal ourselves by forgiving ourselves as well as extending forgiveness to others. Such is the power of redemption and renewal that form the promise of every new year.

Question for Discussion and Reflection: Do you find it difficult to forgive others? Do you find it difficult to forgive yourself and why?

IMPORTANCE OF FRIENDSHIP

Mark: It has been noted that America is suffering from an epidemic of loneliness. Ever since Robert Putnam authored the book, *Bowling Alone*,[1] numerous researchers and demographers have released studies highlighting the erosion of communal institutions—religious communities, fraternal organizations, social clubs, and, yes, even bowling leagues—all of which created a myriad of opportunities for human interaction and sustained contact.

A *Wall Street Journal* article related similar findings on the building of friendships. The results suggested that four in ten Americans claimed to be without a single devoted friend! The article detailed that the critical part of establishing a meaningful friendship was 200 hours of sustained encounters, experiences, interactions, and communication.[2]

Frank, as someone who has had the good fortune of retaining several lifelong friendships, while also creating multiple new ones along the way, what do you make of this epidemic of loneliness and the similar difficulties so many are facing, of living a life without many, or even any, friendships?

Frank: Mark, yes, I have been blessed with good friends, some of whom I met in kindergarten and with whom I continue to enjoy a close and nurturing relationship. The absence of friends in one's life is a fundamental problem. The lack of good friends can lead to a lonely existence which often leads to serious depression. The question is, why is our society filled with lonely people and what can be done about it?

It is not an easy question to answer. I believe, to a large degree that social media keeps people from forming one-on-one interactions, leading to an isolated life, filled with communication that only allows for a mobile phone relationship. Whatever the cause, there is a need to encourage people to put the making of good friends high on their list of priorities.

In 350 BC the Greek philosopher Aristotle listed three types of friendships. The first he labeled as the "Friendship of Utility," which was the kind of friend you find convenient to have in your life. These are the people you work and play with without getting to know each other deeply.

The second type of friendship he called the "Friendship of Pleasure," the friend in your life whom you spend a great deal of your time with, such as at lunches, dinners, sporting events, and social outings. This type of friend is one with whom you may spend casual time, and even share your feelings, but the relationship never evolves into something more serious.

Aristotle called the last type the "Friendship of the Good." This type of friendship is rare, one in which you become soul mates, understanding each other at a fundamental core, one with whom you express your innermost thoughts and feelings. There is nothing that you would not discuss with the "Friend of the Good." There is true respect, trust, and acceptance of this type of friend with an element of love intertwined. We are lucky if we have just a few of these types of friends.[3]

Mark: Frank, what is so sad is that so many people today have *none* of these kinds of friends. The Surgeon General refers to this as an epidemic of loneliness.[4]

You are onto something when you reference the impact of social media on such a large swath of society. We are all guilty of taking part in this to some degree or another. We text in lieu of having an actual person-to-person conversation. We highlight and post only the most happy and exciting images of our lives, which can make others feel as though they can neither relate nor respond in equal measure, nor share equivalent snapshots of pleasure. And most importantly, we substitute the importance of engaging with a community of meaning with an online presence, one which further creates and sustains a strong and increasing sense of isolation.

It is no surprise that so many of our communal institutions are no longer strong nor even sustainable. Friendship involves human interaction, a shared sense of belonging and purpose, and an ability to be at once vulnerable and empathetic to others. In short, it takes effort. Frank, what do you think?

Frank: I totally agree. It is troubling to learn that so many have stopped becoming affiliated with their religious houses of worship. Becoming a member of a church or synagogue is a wonderful way to meet others and to feel a part of a community. That is certainly what I feel every time I attend a function at The Temple or in any other gathering of the Jewish community. I feel as if I am with friends and family.

There was a large and reputable study that showed that families who have someone with a disability (and loneliness can be disabling), have higher quality life scores if they are affiliated with a church or synagogue when compared with similar families that are not affiliated with a religious house of worship.[5] Living an affiliated Jewish life is one effective way to make friends that start with "Friends of Utility," often leading to "Friends of Pleasure," and with luck, finding a few we can call "Friends of the Good."

Mark: Frank, what you are talking about is the strength offered by communities of faith, although it can really be any organization that allows for sustained interaction between the participants. Such communities of meaning require significant investments of time, focus, and active participation.

They require one to show up, not just to meet one's own needs, but rather for the needs of others within that community or congregation. Friendship emerges from these encounters because of a shared level of caring and commitment to the value of each individual and every relationship.

The adage is still true today: the best way to make a friend is to be one.[6] It does not have to be that hard: show interest in another human being and show vulnerability in the sharing of yourself. You will not only enrich your life with friendships; you will enrich someone else's life as well.

Question for Discussion and Reflection: What are the root causes of loneliness in America today? How can we find a cure?

NOTES

[1] Robert Putnam, *Bowling Alone*, (New York: Simon and Schuster 1995).
[2] Clare Ansberry, "They've Been Friends for 60 Years," *Wall Street Journal*, September 4, 2023.

[3] *Understanding Friendship Through the Eyes of Aristotle, in Philosophy the Classical Edition*, Anika Parker, antigonejournal.com/2021/03/understanding-friendship-through-aristotle.

[4] Youri Benadjaoud, "US Surgeon General Warns about the Dangers of Loneliness," ABC News, June 12, 2024.

[5] Thomas L. Boehm and Erik W. Carter, "Family Quality of Life and Its Correlates Among Parents of Children and Adults with Intellectual Disability," *American Journal on Intellectual and Development Disabilities*, no. 124, 2019, 99–115.

[6] Clare Ansberry

WHY THINGS HAPPEN

Frank: Mark, an age-old question of why things happen is one that you and I have often discussed. Is what happens in life predetermined and for a reason, or is what happens merely a random phenomenon? In his extremely popular book, *When Bad Things Happen to Good People*, Rabbi Harold Kushner believed that things happen randomly and that his young son did not die for any reason or that his death was predetermined.[1] People all over the globe read his book and many believed he was correct. I am one of those people.

A good example of this philosophy is found in the movie, *Sliding Doors*.[2] In the movie, actor Gwyneth Paltrow wakes up one morning and leaves her sleeping boyfriend to take a train to work in downtown London. Upon arriving at work, she is notified that she is fired. Clearly upset, she rushes down the subway stairs to board the train back home. As she approaches the train's closing sliding door, the doors shut closed, and she is unable to enter the train. The next scene shows her rushing down the stairs as she had in the earlier scene but this time, she gets her elbow into the closing doors and can enter the train and begin her trip home.

From that moment the scenes are split, depicting how life unfolds when she does not make the train and when she does. In the latter situation, she arrives home to find her boyfriend in bed with another woman and in the former situation, the boyfriend's lover has left, and she misses the encounter. The movie depicts how each of these two scenarios unfolds and drastically changes her life. In so many ways each time we choose one path over another, we are invoking the foundational principle of this movie. Turn left at a traffic light and arrive safely at your destination. Turn right and you are involved in a traffic accident that destroys your life. Decide at the last moment to attend a party and wind up meeting the person who becomes the love of your life.

Most of the time we are unaware of how every choice we make in our daily activities plays a role in our lives, some small and insignificant but others quite large. Brian Klaas states in his new book, *Fluke*, "We control nothing, but influence everything." He also writes, "If every detail of the past created our present, then every moment of our present is creating our future too."[3] Mark, where do you stand on this question of why things happen?

Mark: Frank, I have quite a different take on this than you do. Perhaps it is a more religious one as well.

While I do believe some things are of our own making, or an extension of the choices we make or the decisions we take, I am open to the belief that there is a greater hand in at least some of where the roads in our lives may lead or take us.

There are at least two distinctly separate ways of considering the random occurrences that we may face in life. The first is to simply describe them as coincidences, the random sequences of cause and effect, the result of the choices we make or the situations we create and in which we therefore find ourselves.

But there is a second way to look at those same occurrences or circumstances, and that is to include the possibility—however remote, perhaps—that there may be a Divine hand at play in this, perhaps either gently or firmly guiding us in a certain way, steering us along a specific path, tipping the scales one way or the other in our thoughts and decisions and actions we make and take.

For me, even that possibility of an occasional Divine intervention is enough to both sustain and even strengthen my faith. I think that outlook creates greater opportunities for spiritual growth and meaning in life.

Frank, how would you react to what I have just suggested?

Frank: Actually, I like it very much as it fits my conception of a Divine presence in our lives. I can envision that Divine presence playing a role in how I act and what I do, and the choices I make still being consistent with my view of the randomness of why things happen. We will never know for sure which of these theories are at work in our lives but it is fun to contemplate the nuances of both.

Mark: Within each of us, the past influences the present, and our present influences the future—ours, our community's, and our world's. And somewhere within that chain of our inherited past and our investments in the future, perhaps God also plays a role in giving shape and form to each of the pathways we forge in each of our lives and the lives of others.

The Hebrew word for such divinely directed interventions is Besheret, or that which is "meant to be," as God would wish for it to be. Life can be viewed as rational, predictable, and sensible, or as a series of coincidences and chance occurrences.

Or…perhaps…

For all that can be explained or predicted, there are still moments guided by a greater Presence, beyond any of our abilities to fully comprehend or understand. Those are the true moments of holiness we can experience in life, when God touches our days with sacred worth and meaning, God's hand in ours, guiding us along life's path, towards a more meaningful journey and a more meaning-filled life.

Question for Discussion and Reflection: Is what happens in life predetermined for a reason or merely a random event?

NOTES

[1] Kushner, *When Bad Things Happen*, Vintage, 2004.

[2] *Sliding Doors*, Directed by Peter Howitt (Intermedia and Miramax Films, 1988).

[3] Brian Klass, *Fluke*, (New York: Simon & Schuster, 2024), 30.

LOVE

Frank: Loving and being loved are the most important human emotions of life and a feeling that can enrich lives in countless ways. Uttering the words, "I love you," are clearly the three most powerful words one can communicate to another person. Yet there are types of love that differ from one another. There is instant love, romantic and evolving love, the love of stranger and neighbor, and the love of oneself. Each of these originates and are expressed in dissimilar ways.

Instant love is the love one feels the moment one holds a newborn baby for the first time as well as the feeling a newborn child feels for its mother and father. It could also be a grandchild that evokes that instant feeling of love. It is interesting that the first love mentioned in the Bible in Genesis 22 is parental love. "And He said, take now thy son, thine only son, whom thou lovest, even Isaac, and get thee to the land of Moriah… (Genesis 22:2). Instant love is a feeling that translates into a world of action. Humans and animals alike will sacrifice their lives to save and protect the life of their child. It is a sacrifice that we make without thought or consideration. It is a pure act of instant true love.

While evolved love may have its origin with a growing friendship, it often begins with "chemistry" that we may confuse with a true and enduring love. Many call that lust. That lust then evolves into what some term an obsession which often takes over one's entire life. One is consumed with intense feelings for another person and a desire to be with that person as much as possible and to have that person become an integral part of everyday life. As time moves on and with the proper person, that obsessive feeling evolves into what scientists say is a long-term attachment. It is this long-term relationship that we then call true and enduring love. This true love also involves the elements of respect, pride, and trust.

Mark, you have had to deal with all types of love in your profession as a rabbi. How do you view the issue of love between neighbor and stranger?

Mark: Within the Hebrew Scriptures, in the central book of the Torah, within the portion of Leviticus known as the Holiness Code, we reach the ultimate pursuit challenge to all of humankind: "Thou shalt love thy neighbor as thyself (Leviticus 19:18). The words are easy to read, yet excruciatingly difficult, at times, to achieve.

To love your neighbor as yourself means that we are commanded to love someone completely in our lives, despite their faults and failings, to be able to overlook their shortcomings and to try to ignore those things within them that infuriate or exasperate us. In short, we must be as forgiving of them as we are of our own selves. This is much easier said than done.

But what about the strangers in our midst, those who are different from us, those who look different than us, or who speak a different language than us, who come from a different culture or faith or background than us? What of the foreign born or the immigrant to our shores?

On this the Bible and Jewish tradition are clear: we are commanded to love the stranger among us as one of our own. As we read in Exodus: "You shall not oppress a stranger nor wrong him, for you were strangers in the land of Egypt" (Exodus 22:20) NJPS. The commandment to love the stranger is the single most referenced instruction in the Torah. Tradition records that similar instructions on the treatment of the stranger occur no less than thirty-six times in our sacred text.

This tells us much about the need to extend both the definition of our love for others created in God's image, as well as the extent of that inclusion and embrace of that love. The Exodus story, the journey from bondage to liberation, from slavery to freedom, is not meant for us to enjoy and cherish alone. We retell the story at Passover each year to remind ourselves to treat others—even, and perhaps especially, those who are different from us—with compassion, empathy, and love. We, who have known the bitterness of being treated harshly because we were outsiders, we have a sacred obligation to treat others better than we were once treated, because we know how difficult life can be for those excluded or ignored.

Frank, you mentioned the importance of the love of oneself. Can you expand on what you mean by that? It sounds like it could lead to idol worship, with oneself as the idol to be worshiped above and over God.

Frank: Of all the different qualities and descriptions of love that we have discussed, Mark, the love of God seems the most difficult to explain and expound on. In my discussions with friends about their love of God, we have a variety of ways to describe how we came to the place of loving God.

In that regard, I have my own way of describing my love of God.

The God I believe in is within my human form, embedded in the DNA that God created, and this God helps direct me on a path of goodness and righteousness speaking to me through a "Still Small Voice." Religious leaders from different religions have explained that the path to a meaningful and spiritual life could only be possible if one genuinely loved God. It seems, therefore, that I had only to love myself and that would put me on a path of true understanding, spirituality, and love of others. This love of myself and therefore also God, involves feelings of trust, respect, and pride. I have come to a point in my life where I feel that I have been a trusting and respectful person and that I can justify a feeling of pride in how I have conducted my life. Therefore, I feel love for myself with this love resting on the premise that I also love God. I do not believe this is narcissistic, rather it is the God within me that has created who I am. It was not me alone.

Question for Discussion and Reflection: How do you define love?

"A PERFECT CHILD"

Frank: During my fifty years of practice, I participated in the care of thousands of pregnant women and have attempted to answer the many questions that each patient invariably wants answered. While these questions are often specific to each patient's pregnancy, one common question usually surfaces during this discussion, "Is my baby okay?" Because it is so difficult for me to define "okay," this question has always been a tough one for me to answer.

At the heart of this question lies a pregnant patient's desire to know if her unborn child will be perfect (normal and healthy), a very reasonable concern. Once again, however, defining perfect is not an easy task.

Most pregnant women do not realize that approximately 2% of the four million births each year in this country involve the delivery of a child with a significant congenital defect. That translates to one out of every fifty births! These birth defects include hundreds of diverse types of anomalies such as spina bifida, heart abnormalities, limb deformities, metabolic disorders, and chromosomal abnormalities such as Down syndrome.

When you consider that each of us begins with the union of sperm and egg, which in turn creates one cell, and this one cell continuously divides to create the trillions of cells that result in a living child, it is truly a miracle that any of us are born, much less that we are born perfect. It is with this in mind that I explain to patients that each birth is a miracle and that the uniqueness of each of us is what makes us perfect. I also try to explain that normal is in the eye of the beholder. The gift of life can be "perfect" even in the presence of serious problems.

Mark, I am sure that you have dealt with families whose child was born with problems and needed guidance in how to deal with such a situation. How have you dealt with these families?

Mark: Frank, you have introduced the most sensitive religious topic I can imagine: the worth of each new life, the value of every new soul. Who decides whether that newborn child, or fetus, is "perfect," or "perfect enough," to guarantee both their spiritual sustainability, as well as their physical viability, to then fully welcome their birth as nothing short of a miraculous event in our lives?

Some faiths believe that the decisions whether to choose to bring such a child into the world is not ours to make, that God alone makes that decision. The wisdom offered by these faiths is that God knows us, each of us, individually, before we are even born. As such, each child is of immeasurable worth, each child is created through God's plan and agency, and as such, we are commanded to welcome that child and to nurture them towards maturity, no questions asked, no matter what. It presents every prospective parent with an often heart wrenching decision.

Judaism offers a distinctly different view. The fetus is viewed as a *potential* human life, but *not* a viable, independently functional human being, until the majority of the fetus has emerged from the mother's womb. Only then is it viewed as a complete and viable living being.

The distinction here is a critical one, because it affords each set of parents the ability to be partners with God in making the most painful decision, should their potential child be somehow "not okay," and therefore "less than perfect." The decision as to whether to bring that child into the world, or not, is one that is left up to those parents to make. The choice, in my experience, is never easy: it is among the most brutal, most tough decisions we will ever have to make. Who decides the worth of each life and the value of each soul? How do we reach that determination with a peaceful heart and a comforted conscience? Our Jewish faith can offer couples a path of options to make such a decision easier to make, and certainly easier to bear its consequences.

Frank, your reflections on all of this?

Frank: To let you know my reflections on what you have just written, I must get personal. My son, Tommy, and his wife, Lisa, were expecting twins in 2003—a girl and a boy. I vividly remember the excitement as my wife Julie, and I waited during the delivery and cried with joy as we each held a child in our arms in the recovery room. Marly and Seth were perfect. What dreams and expectations we held for these two precious bundles of joy!

Several hours later, however, we were faced with the fact that Seth had a diagnosis of Down syndrome while his sister Marly did not. Our family was filled with emotions, from the high that came with the birth of the twins to a low at learning about Seth's disability and knowing that he would be different with possible life-long problems.

Later that evening, holding Seth in my arms and gazing into his angelic face, I was overcome with an instant and unconditional love for my grandson. As the tears rolled down my cheek, I understood that despite his diagnosis, to me and those who love him, Seth was a perfect child, to be loved and nurtured, the same as his sister Marly. Our dreams and expectations for him may now be different from those for his sister, yet they are dreams and expectations, nonetheless.

To me, Seth is perfect. As a baby his smile lit up the room and his laughter brought warmth to all who held him. He loved to cuddle and gaze into the eyes of those who held him, and he embraced his sister with what can only be described as pure affection and love. And as he reaches twenty-one years of age, he continues to light up a room with his laughter and bring joy to our hearts every day.

Seth is one of many children who are born every day with birth defects and complications. Yes, his life is filled with challenges, but that is also true of each of us as we embrace life with its difficulties.

As we enter a world in which more genetic information is available for us to consider in defining the "perfect" child, I hope we have room in our world and hearts for those like Seth who are challenged and different, because challenged and different can still be perfect.[1]

Question for Discussion and Reflection: How would you define a perfect child?

NOTE

[1] Dr. Frank Boehm, *Building Patient/Doctor Trust*, (La Vergne, TN: Ingram, 2005) 100–102.

THE TENTH COMMANDMENT

Frank: Mark, I have always been fascinated by the fact that it was the Jewish people who gave the world its first introduction to monotheism as well as laws which God instructs us to follow by giving Moses the Ten Commandments.

I have also noted that, while many of these Ten Commandments are most often quoted, such as "honor the Sabbath, honor your father and mother, thou shalt not murder, steal, commit adultery, or give false testimony," the tenth commandment is not well known, not often quoted, nor well understood. The misunderstood tenth commandment says, "Thou shalt not covet your neighbor's house; thou shalt not covet thy neighbor's wife, nor his maid-servant, nor his ox, nor his ass, nor any thing that is your neighbor's" (Exodus 20:14).

So, I want to ask you, a learned rabbi, what does this commandment mean, and why is it included in this famous giving of laws to the Jewish people?

Mark: Frank, our sages compared the temptation of coveting to a certain type of idolatry. This carries two risks and exposes two vulnerabilities within us.

First, to envy another human being, or to lust after their spouse or to covet their possessions or property, was akin to idol worship, in that we might fall prey to obsessing over our neighbor's possessions or their better lot in life than ours. We come to worship them as opposed to our Creator. Those we envy or covet demand the same things our God would demand of us—namely our time, our focus, and our energy, each in all consuming ways.

Second, and even more importantly, our coveting of others makes us less grateful for our own blessings we possess in each of our own lives. We tend to overlook or even ignore those cherished relationships we should honor, uphold, and safeguard within our own hearts, including those relationships which are sacred to us and to those we love. We become less grateful to God for the gift of each new day we draw breath, and for all the other blessings in our own lives that truly are beyond measure. We come to believe that "the grass is always greener on the other side," all the while discounting and disregarding the bounty of our own harvest.

Frank: I like your explanation, and it makes me wonder why God did not just put as number ten, the commandment, "thou shalt be grateful." By being grateful for what we have we are, in a sense, honoring and thanking God for all we do have in our lives and thereby avoiding envy and jealousy and the desire to have what others have, and we do not.

There is a story that I have always enjoyed telling and that is emblematic of the premise that we should be grateful for what we have in our lives. At a party given by a billionaire friend, Kurt Vonnegut, a famous author tells his friend Joe Heller, also a famous author who wrote the widely read book, *Catch 22*, that their billionaire host made more money in a single day than Heller had earned from his extremely popular book. Heller responded with, "Yes, but I have something he will never have." "What is that?" responded Vonnegut. To which Heller responded, "Enough."[1]

Mark: Frank, you have really hit on the eternal wisdom of the tenth commandment. Envy can destroy our ability to recognize and appreciate the blessings each of us enjoys in our own lives. Jealousy of others can severely mask our ability to be content with our own precious gifts that often lie right before us, even right next to us. There is a difference between ambition for us versus adoration for the achievements of others.

We only have this one life. Why should we spend so much of our time, focus, and energy craving what we covet or envy in the lives of others, rather than cherishing and honoring what we already claim to cherish and enjoy in our own? And here we touch upon the heart of the matter: when we come to covet the relationships that we see in the lives of others, whenever we come to worship them, we do so at the risk of neglecting the relationships of our own. Some may even do so at their own peril, endangering the connection to those closest to them. Some will covet in the most painful of ways: they will violate their obligations to their spouse or other loved ones in pursuit of their neighbor's husband or wife. In doing so, though they may claim to worship God, they are, in fact, bowing down to their own desires, worshiping themselves rather than their Creator.

Frank: No matter how much we have in our lives, there are always others who have more. While it is understandable to seek to increase life's advancements and bounty, it is imperative that we find a way to be grateful for what we have, and that is the overarching message of the tenth commandment. Gratefulness is a virtue that leads to a life of meaning, contentment, and peace and directs us to a path of loving ourselves and thereby loving God.

The first three of the ten commandments address the need to love and honor God, and these commandments are followed by honoring the Sabbath and our parents. The next four deal with specific actions for us to avoid. The last of the ten commandments returns to the demand that we believe in and honor our God, and to do this, we need to be grateful for what we have, all we have done, and all those we have loved. Although it is placed last, it is understandable that God put, "thou shalt not covet" in the top ten.

Question for Discussion and Reflection: How would you define the act of coveting? Is coveting always a terrible thing?

NOTE

[1] Kurt Vonnegut, "Enough," *New Yorker Magazine*, May 2005.

THE SACRED NATURE OF RELATIONSHIPS

Mark: In the Jewish sacred text Pirke Avot, *The Sayings of the Ancestors*, there is a line that speaks to the sacred and transformative potential of meaningful relationships and deep friendships between two or more human souls. The ancient saying goes: "Find yourself a teacher, acquire for yourself a friend."[1]

This is the power that defines true spiritual connection between human souls. It comes from the vulnerability and depth to be found in the exchange of sincere and sympathetic dialogue and discourse shared by those created in the Divine Image, who in turn recognize and affirm that same Image as to be found within each other's souls.

The theologian Martin Buber described this as the "I-Thou" relationship. He suggested that God enters that space shared by the meaningful exchange between two caring human beings, especially those whose friendships affirm life's worth, meaning, and purpose. Such strong, honest, and engaging relationships amplify the meaning of our days, because we demonstrate the fact that the lives of others—including our families and friends—matter in our eyes as well as within our hearts.

Many articles have been written about the loneliness felt by both the young and old. Other articles attest to the fact that the investment in meaningful social interactions and friendships, both new and enduring, can form an antidote to the sense of profound isolation and loneliness. Along the way, these relationships raise the value of the way in which we treasure life itself; they become our greatest possession because of their sustaining ability and enduring worth. Even more, they are regular and constant reminders that God's presence rests directly between caring, sympathetic, and often loving friendships and relationships. They touch something deep within our souls and remind us of the magnificence and sacredness of life itself.

Frank, as one who engenders and cherishes such relationships and friendships, new and old over the years, what do you think of this idea that a window towards holiness and sacredness is to be found among such human interactions?

Frank: Mark, I agree that there is an element of sacredness in those special friendships that transcends our more casual and less intense relationships. I previously discussed the Greek philosopher Aristotle, and his three types of friendships which addresses this point.

I have been lucky to have developed a few sacred friendships throughout my life. What about you?

Mark: While I, like you, have been fortunate in cultivating several "Friendships of the Good," especially in my more mature years, as a rabbi I have learned that the greater gift is to try to view *each* of the three types of friendships, described by Aristotle, as worthy of being sacred. The challenge before each of us is to recognize that *every encounter* we have in our lives—from the checkout clerk to the critical care nurse—can be made into a sacred engagement with another human soul. Every contact can be infused with a sense of holiness if we choose to capture the potential in such moments. In so doing, we invite God's presence into the space between us, each of us sharing that space with an invitation for the Divine Presence to enter it.

The question then is: how exactly can we successfully achieve that ambitious goal? The best way is through listening more attentively to those with whom we interact, as a way of acknowledging their value and their worth to us, especially in those moments when our lives most directly intersect with one another.

Judaism's most important prayer, our most elevated sacred text, expresses this clearly: "Hear, O Israel: The Lord our God, the Lord is One" (Deuteronomy 6:4). It is the urgent plea, the dramatic call for our attention, imploring us to listen, to understand the message still to come.

The question has often been asked: why did God give us two ears but only one mouth? The response and its rationale: so that we should attempt to listen twice as much as we might otherwise choose to speak.

The way to infuse our relationships with a renewed sense of holiness, the pathway to creating friendships and acquaintances that are truly sacred, the best way to invite God's presence into the space between us, is to listen with greater attentiveness, to convey a genuine sense of openness, patience, kindness, graciousness, and awareness in truly comprehending the words shared with us by others with whom we interact.

In taking the time to recognize and affirm their value to us, we also affirm our own value to the God who created us. In recognizing and acknowledging the "Still Small Voice" within them, we amplify and magnify the "Still Small Voice" inside each of us. Together, then, we invite God's presence to enter the sacred space between us, and to bless the lives of each of us and of all of us.

Question for Discussion and Reflection: Do you have a friend of the good? If not, why?

NOTE

[1] Mishnah, Pirke Avot, *The Sayings of the Ancestors*, 1:16.

PAIN AND SUFFERING

Frank: There is a story regarding pain that goes something like this: a man tells his doctor that he experiences acute pain each time he bends his right elbow. He wants to know how this can be treated. His doctor replies, "That is easy, don't do that." While there is humor in this story, pain is not a topic we find humorous.

One of the things I learned watching women give birth is that all of us have quite distinct levels of pain tolerance. In my early years of obstetric training, I placed everyone together in their ability to manage their pain of labor. Those women who screamed the loudest for more pain medication were simply not properly prepared for childbirth while those who tolerated their contractions without much pain medication were better prepared and stronger in their resolve to handle the process of labor and delivery. Today I know I was wrong.

Science has shown us that much of the effect of physical pain on the body is decided by our genetic makeup and that one person's feeling of pain at a level of five is another's perception at a level of ten. One thing we also know is that pain is something all humans will at some time in their lives experience in one form or another. It will be how we handle that pain that determines how we are able to live from day to day with some aspect of relief and hope.

Over the years, I have learned that one aspect of pleasure can be defined as the absence of pain. Pleasure is a condition where the body and mind can experience the world around us and can relax in the comfort and awareness of whatever we are doing. Pleasure allows us to focus on and understand what we are experiencing and what we are doing.

Pain takes all this away. Pain separates us from our ability to focus and to experience the world around us. Nothing matters when we are in severe pain. We can no longer "Be here now, now be here," as the guru Ram Dass once proclaimed as his watch words of how to live a fulfilling life.[1]

Mark, you have dealt with many congregants who were suffering from significant pain. How have you been able to help those whose chronic pain has interfered with their physical, emotional, mental, and spiritual health?

Mark: Frank, did you know that Jews have a blessing that we recite each morning that praises God *even despite* our aches and pains? It says, "Blessed are You, God of the Universe, who sets free the captive." We moan, we groan, yet we nevertheless express our gratitude for the ability to literally move forward, to move along with our days, and our lives *despite* the debilitating pain that might greet us right at the break of dawn, and which may inhabit the length of each day and perhaps even infiltrate the balance of all of our days.

From my years of listening to so many about the pain they are carrying, I have come to understand just how all-consuming and exhausting it can be. I have come to learn how it can rob those who suffer moments of immense joy. It can also diminish their ability to fully be in the moment, because their pain occupies a larger space in their lives than anything else.

I also know that while we most often think of the impact of pain primarily in physical terms, I have spent time with many suffering from serious mental pain or emotional trauma. And sometimes, any of these types of pain and suffering can cause an additional, spiritual pain, as they ask the fair and reasonable question as to why God would do this to them; why God would allow this to cripple their mind, body, or spirit, and finally, why God, despite their prayers and supplications, would not relieve them of their severe struggle or discomfort.

At those times, my role was to acknowledge their pain and to lend them a sympathetic ear. Unfortunately, what I cannot do is alleviate them of their suffering nor free them of their misery.

What I can offer them in my role of rabbi is this: I can tell them that within this sacred space, this sanctuary, which offers a respite for out shattered spirits, we are all wounded in some way or another. Some scars and handicaps are clearly visible; others are hidden from our gaze, and yet the injuries and hurts remain, even and especially those buried deep beneath the surface. What I can tell them is this: in this community of souls, we gather to offer comfort and healing to one another. We do so even as we do not always understand God's actions, or inaction. Yet because we are created in God's image, we extend our hearts and our hands to uplift one another in a most sacred way.

Frank, you once spoke from our pulpit about what you had learned from a bout with profound pain. What did you learn from that experience that you hoped would give comfort or strength to others?

Frank: Mark, when the pain left my body after spinal surgery, I was the happiest and most grateful person imaginable. I also understood the phrase, "And this, too, shall pass."

When you realize that your pain is either gone or minimized, there is a feeling of elation and joy.

There are those, however, who never find relief from pain. For these individuals, I have considerable empathy and only wish that at some point in their lives and with medical advances or physical therapy techniques, they, too, will find an element of relief. All of us who have experienced significant pain are more likely to find an increased level of empathy and may, therefore, be more able to be a more compassionate individual.

Question for Discussion and Reflection: Have you experienced significant pain in your life? How did it affect you?

NOTE

[1] Ram Dass, *Be Here Now*, (San Cristoal, NM: Lama Foundation), 1971.

GROWING OLD

Frank: There is a saying: "Good judgement comes from experience, and experience comes from bad judgement."[1] Now that I am in my eighties, I can truly relate to this saying. There are positive aspects of growing older, and avoiding the mistakes and the missteps of everyday life through experiences is clearly one of them.

The aging process teaches us not only how to act, but also what it is we want in life. While I once had trouble saying no to certain requests, I now find it easier to turn down certain requests. I know the difference between what I will and will not enjoy doing and have learned through experience to find as many moments of pleasure and happiness as possible in the years I have left.

Growing old does present problems of health and well-being. Each of our organs, joints, and muscles, much like a carton of milk, have an expiration date. Yet, these negative aspects of aging are trumped by the many maturing processes of growing old. Aging brings patience, gratefulness, and understanding into one's life and most importantly, brings knowledge of what is important and what is not.

When I interviewed dozens of over 75-year-old individuals for my book, *Is Your Life Successful* I found that when I asked this older group of individuals what they considered to be a successful life, their answers were different from the younger groups. Most listed making a positive impact on the lives of others and having a loving family and good friends as their leading definitions of a successful life. These were followed by loving and being loved, being a moral and ethical person, living by the Golden Rule, being able to deal with adversity, using God's gifts of talent and abilities to benefit others, minimizing the negative influences of mistakes, finding happiness, having had an enjoyable job or career, putting a smile on someone's face, and being content and grateful.[2] These definitions developed through life's experiences over the years. We can be thankful for our bad judgement when we are young. If we learn from our missteps, it can help make us better people with a better understanding of what is important in life.

Mark, what do you think?

Mark: I have found that as I reached my fifties, I had a greater sense of peace within myself and a greater calm in addressing the various issues that I faced. I think at that midpoint of the century mark, we begin to draw upon the wisdom of what we have learned, both by trial and error, over the prior decades of our lives.

With that wisdom comes a greater sense of perspective; a more enhanced and more nuanced understanding of people and the circumstances that life places before them. We certainly become both far less judgmental of others and far more forgiving of ourselves. We are much more accepting of our faults and failings and therefore much less harsh in our awareness and our tolerance in the flaws we find in others.

We take comfort and solace in the gift of the time we have enjoyed thus far during our days on earth. We have had the chance to love deeply, to watch our children reach adulthood, to make rich and rewarding friendships, and to engage in meaningful work. We have had the chance to look back over the years and recognize how richly we have been blessed, perhaps not as equally, as compared to others, but fully, nonetheless.

For me, this takes an extremely grateful and spiritual turn: I am so profoundly appreciative of all with which I have been blessed, and I cannot help but be thankful to God for the multitude of gifts God has given to me. I count the gifts of my marriage, my children, and my rabbinic calling and career among those I cherish most.

The cup of life is therefore neither half empty nor half full. To me, it is overflowing with blessings. I think it can be this way for all of us, should we choose to see it that way. Life may not be perfect; but life is precious, nonetheless.

Frank, you are a full two decades older than me. What have these added years taught you in this regard?

Frank: Mark, despite some physical and mental infirmities that have come with the aging process, these negative events are eclipsed by the wisdom I have gained over the years. I would like to believe that wisdom has helped make me a better person, one who is grateful and appreciative of the life I have lived. It has also helped me understand each of my life's major chapters and what those chapters have meant for me.

The first chapter was the first eighteen years of my life when I lived at home and was nurtured and taken care of by loving parents who helped me believe in myself. I loved those years; they were critical in giving me the confidence to move forward to the next chapters. The second chapter included the years I spent in education at college, medical school, and residency which enabled me to spend my life in a career I loved. That chapter overlapped with the third chapter which included marriage, raising a family, as well as practicing the art and science of medicine. While I often looked back at the wonderful years that made up the second and third chapter, I am content now that I have moved into my fourth and last chapter, retirement. The wisdom that has seeped into my body over the years and now brought peace and appreciation into my life could have only been achieved through growing older.

Question for Discussion and Reflection: Do you believe there are good things that happen to us as we age? If so, what are they?

NOTES

[1] "The Muncie Evening Press" of Muncie, Indiana, 1932 (Newspapercom)

[2] Frank H. Boehm, *Is Your Life Successful?* (Nashville: Turner Publishing Company, 2021), 131–155.

HAPPINESS

Frank: I have always been fascinated with the concept of happiness and what it means. Our founding fathers felt this human condition was so important that they added it into the Declaration of Independence (U.S.,1776), "We hold these truths to be self-evident, that all men are created equal, that they are endowed by their Creator with certain unalienable Rights, that among these are Life, Liberty and the pursuit of Happiness." Happiness means different things to different people and the answer to the question "Are you happy?" obviously depends on a multiplicity of factors.

Using more than forty years of extensive research on happiness, social scientists have found three major sources: genes, events, and values. Researchers at the University of Minnesota have tracked identical twins who were separated at birth, raised in different environments, and found that it is our genetic wiring that accounts for almost half of our state of happiness. To a large degree, therefore, fundamentally happy, or unhappy, individuals get it honestly from their parents.[1]

Studies have also revealed that isolated events in our lives do have a significant impact on our state of happiness with the only problem being that the effects are usually short lived. A pay raise or a new job or reaching a major milestone in life can certainly bring happiness into one's life, yet so many of these events are dulled over time. It appears the quest and hard work to reach a lofty goal may bring more happiness than the actual achievement of that goal.

The third process involved in bringing and increasing happiness into one's life is that of values involving faith, family, and friendships. Mark, how do you define happiness and how do you believe the values in one's life influence a state of happiness?

Mark: The rabbis of old, writing in the Talmud in the first and second centuries, include a section offering words of wisdom. In *"The Sayings of the Ancestors"* (Pirkei Avot), they asked the question, "Who is rich?" This was their response: "The one who is content with their lot."[2]

I believe true happiness has much to do with being content with what one has made of his or her life, and with an ability to view his or her life's journey with a mixture of gratitude and appreciation for what life has given them, despite the inevitable hardships and disappointments that all of us must eventually encounter. Happiness can be defined as an enduring sense of contentment, gratitude, and appreciation for the blessings of life. These may include the ability to give and receive love; the opportunity to pursue meaningful and fulfilling work; sufficient ability to provide food and shelter for oneself and one's family; the gifts of freedom and safety from harm; and certainly, the profound grace to rejoice in moments of celebratory experiences as well as moments of spontaneous joy.

I would therefore suggest two distinct types of happiness: one momentary, even fleeting; the other, enduring, everlasting, and profoundly deep. Both have value; but only the enduring one is invaluable, as the defining notion of creating and sustaining a lifetime of happiness.

Frank: I totally agree with you that happiness can be divided into a momentary or fleeting feeling and a more enduring and deep feeling of contentment which I would call pleasure. Random times of happiness occur in special moments of life, such as the birth of a child, marriage, promotions, achievements, financial gain, religious celebrations, vacations, and a host of other such special events in life. This happiness, however, is often short lived.

Pleasure, on the other hand, brings a prolonged richness and contentment into one's life. Contentment in life is the sum of life's pleasurable moments and experiences, including meaningful work, secure familial bonds of love, and the hope of leaving the world a better place. From this state of contentment will come moments of accelerated pleasure with elements of euphoria and excitement, called happiness, which is why I often say to my friends, "May your life be filled with pleasure and may you be blessed with many moments of happiness."

The question often asked is how one keeps a state of pleasure along with episodes of happiness. The answer lies in family, friends, and faith. Family helps ground us and gives us pleasure through the love we have for them and the love they have for us. This love results in a feeling of pleasure. Family can be the glue that binds us together in a nurturing and supportive fashion.

Friends are a necessary part of life. Friends lend us support, caring, aid, understanding, and companionship. For pleasure to be maintained in life, good friends are vital. The famous baseball player, Ty Cobb, said, "If I had my life to live all over again, I would have done things a little differently. I would have had more friends."[3] And the economist, Alan Krueger, once said, "One of the best ways to increase happiness was to spend more time with friends."[4]

Faith is also an important aspect of feeling pleasure through its ability to allow spiritual needs to be met, as well as to offer us a community of like-minded individuals. This community lends its support in a loving and nurturing manner and allows us to feel pleasure.

Mark, what are your thoughts on this concept of achieving a state of pleasure with episodes of happiness occurring in our lives?

Mark: My thoughts are summed up best in the words of the author and poet Ralph Waldo Emerson (has also been attributed to a poem written by Bessie Anderson Stanley): "To laugh often and much; to win the respect of intelligent people and the affection of children; to earn the appreciation of honest critics and endure the betrayal of false friends; to appreciate beauty; to find the beauty in others; to leave the world a bit better whether by a healthy child, a garden patch or a redeemed social condition; to know that one life has breathed easier because you lived here. This is to have succeeded."[5]

Even more than having succeeded, I would argue, Emerson's words convey the deeper sense of happiness which defines the essence of a life well lived. Looking at life through this lens, we can be grateful for each day: at peace with our past, content in the present moment, hopeful for the future.

The words of Rabbi Jacob P. Rudin state it best and succinctly: "When we are dead, and people weep for us and grieve, let it be because we touched their lives with beauty and simplicity. Let it not be said that life was good to us, but rather, *that we were good to life.*[6]

To say that, and to have that said about us, is the most validating, most honest, and most enduring example of having lived a pleasurable, happy, and meaningful life.

Question for Discussion and Reflection: How do you define happiness? How does the achievement of happiness affect your life?

NOTES

[1] Thomas Bouchara, "Minnesota Twin Study," *Science*, October 12, 1980.

[2] Mishnah, Pirke Avot, *The Sayings of the Ancestors*, 4:1.

[3] Anthony J. Connor, *Voices from Cooperstown: Baseball Hall of Fame*, (New York: Galahad Books, 1998), 286.

[4] David Leonhardt, "David Leonhardt Newsletter," March 19, 2019.

[5] Ralph Waldo Emerson, "To Laugh Often and Much," also attributed to Bessie Anderson Stanley, "To Laugh Much and Often," 1905.

[6] Rabbi Jacob Phillip Rudin, *Gates of Prayer for Weekdays and at a House of Morning*, ed. Chaim Stern, (New York: Central Conference of American Rabbis, 1992), 36.

SECTION THREE

Facing Our Future Challenges with Faith

AWARENESS

Frank: Mark, over the years, I have learned that awareness impacts the definition of a meaningful life. Without awareness we are limited in our ability to adequately view the world around us, to see its beauty and richness, and to fully embrace the moment in which we are living. Awareness and being present are critical in helping us enrich our lives.

Many years ago, I met a patient who taught me an important lesson on awareness being a critical ingredient of happiness and living a meaningful life. I was seeing patients in a cancer clinic at the City of Hope Hospital in California when I walked into one of the rooms and sat down to speak with a middle-aged woman who had advanced metastatic breast cancer. The tumor had spread to her lungs, making it difficult for her to speak. Words came slowly and only with significant effort, and while we had spoken before on other visits, our times together had been perfunctory and businesslike. As we sat together in that small examining room, I sat back in my chair and, speaking softly, inquired as to how she was doing. Her response still echoes in my mind today as she uttered with a smile, "Wonderful." Somewhat taken aback, I remarked how interesting it was that such cheerfulness filled her at a time of such obvious illness. She replied, "The best thing that ever happened to me, Doctor, was the day I was told I had cancer."

"How could that be?" I asked. "Well, Doctor," she replied. "Before I knew I had cancer, I never saw the sun rise or set, and I was never aware of all the wonderful things life had to offer. I went through each day on auto-drive, much like the times I drove home from work but was unaware of the drive until the moment I pulled into my garage. But since that day, knowing my days were limited and therefore precious, I noticed the sunset and the sunrise. I heard sounds I had never heard before. I smelled fragrances, tasted food, and touched textures as never before. Most importantly, I hugged my loved ones with an intensity that brought forth feelings of real joy. All at once I became alive and a richness filled my every day."

With eyes slightly moist, I finished my exam and as I turned to leave, she said, "Just think of it, Doctor. You could start all that today, without cancer." Three weeks later she took her last breath and died peacefully in her hospital bed. As I pulled the sheet over her placid face, I knew that a great lesson was given to me by this thoughtful woman—one that I would never forget.[1]

Mark: Frank, the touching story you shared is a reminder to all of us to value and cherish each day of life, to take nothing for granted, including those we love, and to find reasons to give blessing for every opportunity we are given to enjoy life.

I am reminded of the old rabbinic teaching in which people are instructed to carry two different scraps of paper in each of their front pockets during every day of their lives. While each text held a reference to a verse of scripture, they were opposite yet balanced in the perspectives which they offer to us.

The first slip of paper had the words, "For my sake was the world created." The second, had written upon it, "I am but dust and ashes." These two pieces of paper served as daily reminders of the majesty of each of our lives, the possibilities that we were able to enjoy as creations of God. However, they also reminded us of our finiteness, of the limit to our days, and the need therefore to make use of them, to appreciate each of them, and to be grateful for the gifts of those days, those precious days, lent to us to enjoy, to celebrate, and to cherish.

It is important, therefore, to develop and sustain an attitude of gratitude. Even more, it is critical that we foster a sense of humility, mindful of the preciousness and the sanctity of every day, of every experience, and every interaction with other human beings whose lives we touch.

Frank, these thoughts resonate with the story you shared. I am curious about what else you might have to contribute that might enhance this reminder to all of us to live our lives most fully and with a more complete sense of awareness.

Frank: Unfortunately, many of us too often go through life with much the same experience. We work and play yet are not truly aware of our surroundings or any real aspect of the experience itself. We do not savor the moment and, therefore, cannot bring awareness to a suitable level. In other words, we often go through life much like that car ride, suddenly finding that life is over, and we had not been aware of the journey, unable to genuinely enjoy and bring awareness and richness to our lives.

Too many of us have difficulties living in the present. We glorify the past and look to the future to give us pleasure or peace. In fact, the good old days are now, not then nor necessarily in the future. We can and should become more aware of each moment of our lives. We must awaken from our sleepwalking by sharpening our senses so that we can view the beauty of nature that surrounds us, savor the taste of the food we eat, smell the wonderful fragrance of flowers, feel the wind on our face and the love of family and friends that surround us. In this way, we will not remain unaware of our drive through life. We can feel that we have lived a truly meaningful and fully present life.

Question for Discussion and Reflection: Do you feel as if you are living in the present? Are you aware and appreciative of your surroundings? If not, what can you do to change that?

NOTE

[1] Frank H. Boehm, *Doctors Cry, Too*, (Carlsbad, CA: Hay House Publishing, 2001), 37.

BEING BOTH

Frank: Mark, with over 70% of our Reform Jewish young adults marrying someone of a different faith, the Reform movement has been confronted with requests from some of these interfaith couples to allow their children to alternate weekly attendance at their synagogue's Religious School with a similar experience at a Christian Sunday School. These are couples who are raising their children with a "Being Both" religious experience.

Currently, many Reform congregations do not give permission for this every other week exposure to both Judaism and Christianity. What are your thoughts?

Mark: Frank, you are asking a fundamental question that challenges the limits and the boundaries of the inclusive sense that Reform Judaism has always sought to embrace. This ultimate question goes to the very heart of who we consider to be a Jew, or who we consider to be Jewish enough.

We Reform Jews have always stretched our comfort levels for the sake of our senses of inclusion and embrace. We have done so with interfaith couples; same sex couples; Jews by choice; Jews of color; and Jews of various sexual orientation and identification. We have done so with the primary concern of being Judaism's easiest entryway to a meaningful, loving, and accepting Jewish community. We should consider creating a similar path for these "Being Both" families. Do we really wish to exclude them? Are they really a threat to what we claim to value and who we claim to be? Does their potential exclusion weaken or strengthen us?

Even the Hebrew Union College, the seminary of the Reform Movement, has acknowledged and accepted this reality. If the seminary now opens its doors to dual faith couples, shouldn't Reform Temples open their doors and religious school classes, as well?

Frank: According to an ancient tradition, a rabbi should turn away a potential candidate for conversion to Judaism up to three times to assess the candidate's sincerity. While most rabbis no longer adhere to this rule, there are often obstacles in the way for an individual to be considered Jewish.

This rule of not allowing children of a mixed religious family to study Judaism while also attending Sunday School every other week is one of those obstacles and will result in that child never accepting Judaism as their religion later in life.

To answer your question, I believe that this exclusion will weaken our religion, not strengthen it. What are we so worried about? There are only sixteen million Jews in a world of eight billion people, making us approximately 0.2% of all people on earth. Surely, we have room in our schools and in our hearts to expose these "Being Both" children of interfaith marriages to the beauty and wonder of Judaism.

We need to revisit policies of exclusion and move to one of inclusion. One way is to consider the following suggested guideline for Reform Congregations to consider: a child of an interfaith marriage, whose parents want their child to experience an education in both a Jewish and non-Jewish religious education, is welcomed to attend Jewish Religious School on an alternative weekly basis during the school year. However, any such child whose religious participation includes both Jewish and non-Jewish education, and who wishes to take part in Jewish life cycle events such as Bar and Bat Mitzvah, must adhere to established guidelines or policies as set forth by the clergy and officers of that congregation. Mark, what do you think?

Mark: Frank, there is real wisdom in the idea you have put forward. The reality is that the next generations of Reform Jews will no doubt include more dual faith households in terms of the active religious participation of both parents. Whether we would prefer it to be this way, or not, makes no difference in the decisions these couples and families will make. It is what it is, and we may either respond to this reality with our full embrace of these families and their children, or we can choose to close the door to them, losing them for a long time, perhaps forever. Is that really the best choice we wish to make?

I believe in the product we offer, the warmth and the wisdom of our Jewish traditions and beliefs. I would like to give a full demonstration and education of our faith to every family who wishes for their child to be exposed to it.

At the end of the day, if we are strong in our own Jewish identity as Reform Jews, and if we stay true to our ideals of inclusion and embrace, then what do we have to lose, in comparison to all we might gain?

Question for Discussion and Reflection: Should Jewish institutes allow children of interfaith marriages to obtain both a Jewish and non-Jewish education? Why?

CLOSURE

Frank: As a physician who has taken care of many patients who have dealt with a grieving process following the loss of a loved one, I have formed several opinions on how some individuals attempt to heal a broken heart. While many may label this point in time as closure, I disagree. Let me explain.

Several definitions of closure are found in dictionaries and literature. One says, "A situation in which something closes forever, as well as a feeling that something has been completed or that a problem has been solved."[1] This definition does not fit when dealing with grief. Rather, I believe in a definition that better defines closure in the grieving process. It is a feeling that a terrible experience such as a death of a loved one has reached a point where one can start to live again in a calm and normal way. However, even that definition does not acknowledge the fact that when we are devastated by loss it never totally leaves our waking moments and there is never true closure, only the lessening of pain and anguish.

Patients have told me that following their loss, while people thought what they were saying was helpful, they instead made comments that were quite painful, even causing anger. Such statements as, "You are young and can have more children," "It was meant to be," or "It was God's will," are not helpful even if the intent is to be sympathetic. Another statement that often causes anger is, "I know how you feel." Patients tell me that "They do not know how I feel, and it hurts to hear such comments."

Then there are those who have expressed how discomforting it was to hear from individuals that time will heal their pain, and that closure will eventually come, when in fact there is never closure from grief. What comes are memories and feelings of love that become a part of our daily lives and help sustain us as we strive to move forward. The only words one should utter to a grieving person are, "I am so sorry."

Mark, you have had numerous congregants over the years who have dealt with this issue of closure following the death of a loved one. What are your thoughts on my comments?

Mark: Frank, I believe, like you, that much of what we say to others often reflects our own fears and vulnerabilities regarding the terminal illness of a relative or friend. This is often followed by a similar discomfort and awkwardness in the way in which we often address those who are in mourning over the loss of that loved one.

Our fears with regards to the tentativeness of each of our lives—our temporary time on this earth—cause us to say things or to parrot things we have heard others say that we believe might offer comfort, even if we do not believe in them ourselves. In offering up such remarks, like the ones you previously mentioned, we offer no comfort at all to the mourners, and, in fact, we may even, if unintentionally, magnify their pain upon hearing such comments.

What we need to understand is that their loss is not only real for them, but it is permanent as well. Therefore, nothing we can say, for example, that "They are closer to God now," or "They are in a better place," none of these phrases will bring them comfort. Those who mourn the loss of a loved one are, as the Psalmist said, walking in the valley of the shadow of death. No words can heal their hearts.

Except these phrases: "I am sorry for your loss. You lost such a good soul. I am here for you whenever you need me. May his or her memory be a blessing." We should let our presence at their side, or at the graveside, or at the shiva minyan (seven days of at home mourning with family and friends), speak for us. In fact, it speaks volumes as to the worth of the mourner's relationship to us, which our presence will demonstrate and which will endure beyond this moment of profound loss.

Some are so fearful of saying the wrong thing that they choose to say nothing. Some are so gripped by their own fear of death that they stay away entirely, trying to shield themselves from the potential trauma of attending a funeral or standing at the graveside.

My years of such encounters, both personal and professional, have taught me a few things. First, show up to offer support and comfort. Second, choose your words carefully and selectively when addressing the mourner; let your presence at their side speak for you. Third, let the warmth of your touch, and the comfort and strength offered by your embrace, add even more to the message of sympathy you might wish to convey. Fourth, continue to show up for them, right beside them, long after the immediacy of their loss. Fifth, and finally, take the time to reflect on the meaning of the phrase "May those we have lost be remembered as a blessing." Reflect on some specific examples of those blessings of their lives which they have left as a legacy to their loved ones. Because someday that is how others will remember us.

Question for Discussion and Reflection: How have you dealt with the loss of a loved one? Can there ever be closure of grief and sadness?

NOTE

[1] Britannica, http://www.britannica.com>dictionary>closure.

A SUCCESSFUL LIFE

Frank: Years ago, I began asking myself if my life was successful. The first answer was that, of course, I was successful. I was a physician, had raised three children who had good careers and who were all happily married and wonderful parents to our nine grandchildren. I had a loving, incredibly happy marriage of over three decades and close, loving friends. What more was there? Still, after all the years and all I had experienced, I wondered if my life was truly a successful one. I needed a good definition. The more I thought about it, the more I was intrigued by the thought that there must be a wide spectrum to the definition of a successful life. I believed that the answer to my question was heavily nuanced and would be dependent upon the many aspects and measures of an individual's life.[1]

Our individual definitions are unique to our experiences in life and our age, just as our DNA is a biological and specific signature for each of us. I concluded that a successful life would be one in which an individual believed that they had either maximized their genetic potential and environmental influences or had been able to minimize or overcome negative aspects of their genetic inheritance and environmental influences. This simple, objective, and generic definition seemed to allow for an egalitarian approach to defining a successful life. This definition would allow for individuals to feel as if their lives had indeed been successful, unlike Webster's definition which says that success is "accomplishing an aim or purpose, having achieved popularity, profit, or distinction."[2] In addition, I added subjective definitions to a successful life such as loving and being loved, having dear friends, having work that is meaningful, helping make the world a better place, and having religious faith in life to name just a few.

We all want to feel as if our lives have purpose and meaning and that we will be remembered as someone who contributed in some manner to the well-being of the world we lived in. That well-being includes sharing love and support of family, helping the sick, comforting the depressed, aiding the homeless, feeding the hungry, clothing the naked, and a host of other noble activities that exemplified the sharing of one's resources, time, and effort.

Mark, how do you define a successful and meaningful life?

Mark: Frank, I love the way you have answered this question. I think the mistake people make is in their desire to place happiness above meaningfulness. As I see it, we all wish for lives filled with joy and delight, celebration, and exaltation. But the search for happiness alone does not guarantee a meaningful or a successful life. On the other hand, Judaism affirms that a life filled with meaning, in service to something higher than oneself, along with caring for the needs of others, can lead to and create opportunities and occasions for true happiness and immeasurable joy.

To me, that is a more spiritual way of defining a successful life, a life that makes significant use of the blessings which God has given to each of us. If you are actively grateful for all you have been blessed with in your life; if you are able to be thankful for every day; if you are able to measure yourself by the advancements you have made from the beginning to the end of your life; if you are able to respond to adversity in a consistently positive manner at each crossroad and challenging chapter of your life; if you have lived a life filled with love and loving relationships measured in tangible acts and expressions of that love for others; and if you have fashioned a life that brings blessings to others, to all those whom you encounter and embrace throughout your life; then I believe you will have lived a successful life.

Frank, what is your response to someone who has struggled through various times in their lives and may question whether their life was worthwhile, fulfilling, or successful? Not everyone has been blessed or perhaps as privileged to view their time on earth as meaningfully as you or I. What would you tell them in terms of a better way to view their experience in living a life worth living?

Frank: Mark, as we age, it becomes increasingly clear what our definitions of a successful life are and whether we have or have not led a successful life. For a variety of reasons, however, not everyone believes that they can achieve a successful life. There are obstacles in their path they feel may impede their ability to feel as if their lives have been worthwhile and meaningful. However, even with interfering obstacles, there are ways for us to create a definition that works for the life we have lived.

A life of illness can still be a life filled with friends and faith. A life of disability can still be a life filled with gratefulness and pride in what one has been able to do. A life of loss or sorrow can still be a life filled with helping others and making this world a better place. A life of poverty can still be a life filled with pride by raising children who accomplish a life of success on their own, and a life of unfulfilling employment can still be a life filled with family, friends, and faith.

The bar for living a successful life need not be a high one. A world in which there are vast numbers of individuals from young to old, from rich to poor, from laborer to professional, from religious to atheist, from parent to childless, from gifted to average, and from healthy to compromised, is a world that values the total worth and vast differences of all human beings in a most egalitarian manner. When the time comes for our lives to end, we should be able to appropriately evaluate our lives as successful or not.

The objective and subjective definition of a successful life I have referred to should, after careful evaluation of the life we have led, lead us to the conclusion that we have, indeed, lived a most successful life.

Question for Discussion and Reflection: What is your definition of a successful life?

NOTES

[1] Frank H. Boehm, *Is Your Life Successful?* xiii.
[2] Merriam Webster, http://merriamwebster.com>successful.

JEW HATRED

Frank: Mark, as we are currently witnessing an enormous rise in antisemitism in this country and around the world, I have been thinking about this issue daily. It is so exceedingly difficult for me to understand the reasons why so many people throughout history have found it plausible and reasonable to hate Jews. What about our paltry number compared to the world's population has caused this aversion to our people? While I have read theories about the reason for this prejudice and hatred, none is a sufficiently sustaining nor dominant reason.

Sure, we are a successful and well-educated people and God's chosen, as well as representing "the other" in societies where Jews live; and yes, the high priests in Jerusalem were complicit in giving Pontius Pilot the go ahead to crucify Jesus. But do any of these explain history's long and pervasive aversion to the children of Israel? We are not all so extraordinarily successful or educated and often we question if we are really the chosen people.

I have been impressed with the argument made by some that societies have become infected with a virus, or a cancer of antisemitism, and that virus or cancer mutates or metastasizes over time depending on what is considered virtuous in that society and then blames the Jew for being opposite of that virtue.

Mark, what do you think of this explanation for antisemitism?

Mark: Frank, I do believe there is really something valid in comparing antisemitism to a chronic, incurable disease, like some elusive cancer, or mysterious virus, each with remedies to reduce the impact or extent of the illness, yet without any successful way to totally cure the patient or eradicate the infection. It does make sense that a society's perceived virtue sets the stage for blaming the Jew for standing for the very opposite of that virtue.

Frank: Right. For instance, in a society that considers religion to be the dominant virtue of its people, leaders of that society use antisemitism to describe the Jew as the killer of God. Every society needs an "other" to take the blame for the problems of that society. For a society that is capitalistic, the Jew is labeled as a hated communist; and for a communistic society, the Jew is hated as a capitalist.

In today's America, the virtue of our society is on the emphasis of human rights, anti-racism, and equality. So many in our country are blaming the Jews as being the exact opposite representation of these virtuous principles. Jews are said to violate human rights of Palestinians and in that way are showing bigoted, racist, and apartheid behavior.

In other words, antisemitism acts much like a virus or cancer, continuing to evolve and adapt to new circumstances and conditions, but never totally going away.

Do you believe that there is a treatment for this historical hatred for Jews?

Mark: Well, if there is a cure, it is yet to be discovered despite two thousand years of searching for it. But, Frank, you are trying to use logic for a hatred that has consistently defied rational explanation. People hate Jews for so many reasons.

The church spent centuries trying to convert us, or expel us, or torture us, or extinguish our existence. Various governments or dictators have concluded that we are the disease which they need to eradicate from their midst by eliminating or expelling or executing our people. There are those on the far right who think we are trying to replace their certain way of life. And there are now those on the extreme left who view us as occupiers, colonialists, and oppressors.

So long as there have been Jews, there has been the cancer of antisemitism. There is no cure. All we can do is educate others and defend our rights and civil liberties.

And now that there is a Jewish homeland, we can finally utilize the infusion of Jewish strength and power: there now is a Jewish army that can function as the first responder to defend the Jewish people from any further attack or assault of the virus of Jew hatred.

Frank, does this answer your question? You have been on this earth longer than I have. Do you believe there is a remedy to be found there?

Frank: Thanks for reminding me that I am twenty years older than you and yes, it does satisfy my question because there is no cure for antisemitism. It will continue in the hearts of many throughout the world despite all attempts through history to eradicate it. No vaccine of education or good will and no chemotherapy of assimilation will be effective. But for the first time in history there is an antidote. An antidote is defined as a substance taken to counteract a particular poison. The poison in this case is antisemitism and the antidote is the State of Israel combined with two words that arose from the ashes of the six million Jews who perished in the Holocaust, "Never again."

Never have we had these two words of "never again" backed up by an extremely powerful nation for Jews. This is our antidote, and it is our salvation. Antisemitism will live forever, but so will we Jews, thanks to the State of Israel and the two words which changed all that we have previously had to endure.

Question for Discussion and Reflection: What do you think are the root causes of Jewish hatred?

JEWISH VISION

Frank: We have all heard the question, "If a tree falls in a forest and no one is there to hear it fall, does it make a sound?" The answer is no. The making of sound requires two physics principles; an event that creates sound waves and a receiver to register and amplify those sound waves thus creating audible sound.

If we, as a Jewish people, do not hear the sound waves of hatred once again filling our world, we will not have the vision to act with foresight and wisdom. We must have the vision to educate ourselves. We need to read books, newspapers, magazines, and Internet news and attend seminars, lectures, and classes about Israel history and its current affairs. We need to understand the complexities of the world and the environment Israel is living in. If we do not, we will have failed to hear the sound waves of Jewish anguish throughout the world. We need to use the tools of facts, and these tools can be used as weapons to help battle ignorance, lies, untruths, and myths that permeate current discourse about Israel. The act of Jew hatred currently gathering momentum around the world is often disguised as anti-Zionism, creating a concept that grows daily in strength and volume throughout the world.

Jews spread throughout the world must maintain support for Israel, as well as a commitment to teach ourselves and our children the rich history and truth of Israel and the Jewish people so that when global Jewish hatred rears its ugly head, as it is doing now, we will have a response that is based on understanding, history, and fact. This may not be enough to stem the tide, but we can at least make the effort. Too much rides on the survival of Israel and the future of the Jewish people.

Mark, in your opinion, what else do we, as a Jewish people, need to do to gain the vision needed in today's world of growing Jew hatred and anti-Zionism?

Mark: Frank, we need to begin by reminding ourselves, and the world, about our incredible and enduring resilience as a people and as a faith. The strength of that resilience is embedded in the Jewish DNA that defines us as a people. It has propelled us past pogroms and persecutions; it allowed us to survive despite blood libels against us and discriminatory practices that have tried to systematically limit us and our aspirations as individuals and as a people. Think about it: in the face of the darkest of times, we have nonetheless produced the brightest of minds and the most successful of pursuits in every professional realm. Is it a mere coincidence, or a real surprise, that we, a small fraction of the world's population, have produced a large and disproportionate number of Nobel prize winners?

My father, of blessed memory, often told me of the comparison of the Jewish people to an egg submerged in boiling water: the longer you cook it, the harder it gets. We have learned to survive against all odds, and to thrive despite all obstacles set before us. This is our starting line. It is by no means our finish line.

We are a people of unwavering hope. We Jews are the people whose national anthem is Hatikvah—the Hope. We pray for a brighter day, even in the darkest of times.

Remember, we are the people challenged to forever be "A light unto the nations" (Isaiah 49:6). With those flames of hope, we keep the darkness at bay.

We need to be mindful that Judaism is a religion of joy and celebration of the human spirit. A Jew, according to tradition, is instructed to offer a hundred blessings each day, to celebrate and elevate life's most positive and uplifting moments, both big and small. We believe in that approach to life, to conquering despair with buoyancy, to utilizing an optimistic spirit as the best antidote to the pessimism that so often burdens and darkens our world and worldview.

Finally, a story from our tradition, one that relates as well to the current day: there is a ring worn by the wise souls among us that says, "Gam zeh yaavor," the Hebrew phrase meaning "This, too, shall pass." The words are both a calming message and a cautionary tale as well. In the worst of times, try to remember that they, too, shall pass. But the warning is also not to get too comfortable, too at ease with one's surroundings, because those times, too, will also pass. Such is the reality of our Jewish existence. Our status is always in flux, our residence in a particular place is only temporary.

Which brings us to the shock many of us feel as Jews in America right now: we are puzzled, disturbed, frightened, and alarmed by the rise in antisemitism in a land we thought was immune to it. And most disconcerting, it comes not just from the far right, but now from a broad section of the left. It comes from groups with whom we thought we shared a similar path to the pursuit of shared goals of social justice and equal rights for all minorities, including us.

So Frank, two questions for you: first, you use the term Jew hatred instead of antisemitism or anti-Zionism to describe this surge of antipathy towards us now. Why have you decided to introduce that term? Second, are you still optimistic about our future as Jews, in America, in Israel, and throughout the world?

Frank: While antisemitism is thought to be a watch word for Jew hatred, it should be noted that a Semite is a member of any of the peoples who speak or spoke a Semitic language, including Jews and Arabs. Let us be more exact and correct; Jew hatred is more descriptive and appropriately inclusive and that is why I choose to use the term Jew hatred rather than antisemitism.

As to your second question of whether I am optimistic about the Jewish future, let me say, yes, I am. Nonetheless, I remain worried about Israel's ability to continue the fight against their enemies. I am emboldened that Israel has nuclear weapons and that it still has America as its biggest ally. My hope is that, as it has happened before, Israel will continue its existence despite its enemies and will continue to be a homeland for the Jewish people.

The people of Israel want nothing more than peace with its neighbors, yet peace stays elusive and a growing hatred for Israel and the Jewish people is spreading throughout the world. History has taught us that Jews represent the canary in the coal mine often being the first victims but not the last. It was Pastor Martin Niemoeller who said it best as he explained what had happened with the Nazis: "First they came for the Communists, but I was not a Communist, so I did not speak out. Then they came for the Socialists and the trade Unionists, but I was neither, so I did not speak out. Then they came for the Jews, but I was not a Jew, so I did not speak out. And when they came for me, there was no one left to speak out for me."[1]

It is my hope that as we Jews hear the sound of bigotry, hatred, and violence rising in America, we have the vision to arm ourselves with weapons of facts and stand strong in our resolve to combat the oldest of all hatreds, Jew hatred.

Question for Discussion and Reflection: What can Jews do to combat the Jew hatred that is increasing throughout the world today?

NOTE

[1] Martin Niemoller, "Speech to Confessing Church," Frankfurt, Germany, 1946.

JEWISH AMERICAN OR AN AMERICAN JEW?

Frank: Mark, many years ago my father, of blessed memory, told me that since his entire family were Germans dating even before Germany became a unified country in 1871, he had always considered himself to be a Jewish German rather than a German Jew. Then Hitler came to power in 1933 and changed that. In 1935 my father's German citizenship was taken from him and the rest of German Jews and life became so unbearable that he and my mother left Germany to come to America, where he became a citizen and lived the rest of his life in comfort and peace.

Recently, with all the turmoil that has existed in Israel and the Middle East and the rise of antisemitism in America, I began to ponder that same question my father asked himself so many years ago. Was I an American Jew or a Jewish American? I began asking friends this question and most, but not all, said that they felt they were Jewish Americans. I wonder what your thoughts are on this question.

Mark: Frank, the memories you share of your father's prescient sense of the inevitable rise of and domination by the Nazi Party, and what that would mean for the Jews of Germany and all of Europe, shows astonishingly keen insight, and a profound and amazing courage to escape when he did. I am afraid that there is a very real sense among Jewish Americans right now of that history repeating itself, right here, right now, even in this exceptional land that has loved and welcomed us, and which we have come to love and embrace as well.

Once again, Jews have become a target of hate, in an ever increasing and exponential fashion. The antisemitism we have come to expect from the far right ("The Jews shall not replace us!") has been joined now by those on the far left, including those groups we thought were our allies and friends. And, since the devastating massacre in the Jewish homeland on October 7, 2023, we have seen a surge of both violent rhetoric and violent actions directed towards Jewish people across the globe, including within our own country's borders.

All of which has caused us to ask the question you initially raised: what are we—each of us—Jewish Americans or American Jews?

Frank, what is the difference between the two, at least as far as you define it?

Frank: I always considered myself to be a Jewish American and I was equally secure with both identities. However, with a significant and disturbing rise in antisemitism in our world and especially in this country, I am rethinking my answer. History's tale of how Jews have been treated in other countries is on my side.

Antisemitism is as old as history itself and dates to ancient times: Jews were expelled during the time of the Assyrian and Babylonian Kingdoms as well as from Rome in 139 BCE, 50 CE, and 135 CE.

- Jews were thrown out of Italy in 19 CE and from North Africa in the tenth century.

- In more modern times, Jews were expelled from England in 1290, France in 1306, and 1394, Spain in 1492, Portugal in 1496, Russia in the fifteenth century, Lithuania in 1495, Germany and North Italy during the fourteenth to sixteenth centuries, Ukraine in 1648 and 1915, and Prague in 1744.
- And from the Arab countries of Egypt, Lebanon, Syria, Iraq, Yemen, Libya, Morocco in 1948.
- And, of course, there is Germany in 1935.

It would seem, therefore, that even America may someday follow in history's footprint and make life here difficult if not impossible for Jews. With that in mind, I am aware that I am a Jew and will always be a Jew, no matter what happens to our wonderful America. Someday, however, I may not be able to consider myself an American and I cannot say that what happened to my father, could not also happen to me. So, in response, when asked if I am a Jewish American or an American Jew my response is a resounding, I am an American Jew!

How would you respond to this same question?

Mark: Frank, you've made the case for the historical record that none of us wants to hear nor heed: that in every single country in which Jews have ever lived, they were either expelled, exterminated, or erased from any continuous presence in any land in which they attempted or assumed they had found a safe haven or harbor.

This is the cruel fact that we must recognize as Jews living in this country as well. While America has been a land of opportunity for our people, and continues to be so, the rise of antisemitism—both on the right as well as now increasingly on the left, has shaken and frightened many of us with good reason.

Today, we are still secure, living in a country in which we have thrived and distinguished ourselves like in no other place, in no other time in our history. And we, in turn, have contributed to the welfare of this Golden Land on an unparalleled scale and degree.

Tomorrow, who knows what will happen? The reality of Jewish history is such that no matter where we have lived, there is always a time limit on our welcome. I hope and pray that such a time may be a long time away from now, but the possibility of exile, even here, is not beyond comprehension.

So, while I love this country, without question and without end, I love my Judaism and my Jewish heritage and faith even more. Therefore, when push comes to shove, Frank, I will always consider myself an American Jew, as well, just like you: I will always choose to highlight my Jewish identity, even over my pride in being an American.

Question for Discussion and Reflection: Do you consider yourself an American Jew or a Jewish American? Why?

HEALTHCARE: A RIGHT OR A PRIVILEGE?

Frank: In the fifth century B.C. one of the oldest documents in history was written by Hippocrates and involved a code of ethics for the practitioner of medicine. While this code of ethics has changed over the years to fit more modern times, it still is one of the only such codes for a profession.

The code of medical ethics highlights four basic principles: beneficence, non-maleficence, autonomy, and justice. Beneficence relates to doing good for patients while non-maleficence relates to refraining from doing harm. In today's language that is viewed in the context of the risk benefit ratio of medical care. Autonomy is the principle that relates to a patient having a sacred right to make decisions about medical care that is offered, while justice is the equal dispensation of the benefits (healthcare) and burdens (costs) of healthcare.

In America today, we seriously violate this last ethical principle of justice every day by not having a system of universal healthcare as all other comparable countries throughout the world have. This lack of healthcare insurance exists today for 9% Americans with another 23% being under insured. Statistics reveal that when these patients present for medical care, their disease and condition are often more advanced, and they experience a worse outcome including higher mortality rates.

In addition, of the hundreds of thousands of bankruptcies in this country each year, the majority are due to medical expenses, a situation that does not exist in any other country. We have a problem with the ethical issue of justice when it comes to healthcare in America, and I believe this to be a moral issue that is heavily involved in religious doctrine.

Mark, what do you believe are these religious doctrines that we violate in America by the absence of universal healthcare, and do you believe healthcare is a right or a privilege?

Mark: Every faith tradition values the preservation of human life as its highest moral value. In Hebrew we refer to this as "Pikuach Nefesh" (the saving of a human life): it is a commandment for which every other commandment can be set aside.

Judaism shares this point of view, that every life is sacred and that, therefore, access to adequate healthcare is a fundamental human right. It is not a privilege left only to a certain few. Rather, it is incumbent on society to extend an equal amount of sufficient medical care to all who require it.

The earliest recorded prayer we know of in Western civilization comes from the biblical text, found within the Book of Exodus. Moses implores God to intervene in the treatment of his sister Miriam's suffering: "O God, please heal her now" (Numbers 12:13).

But prayers alone, while powerful, are not in and of themselves enough, neither to heal nor to cure those who are ill. For that, medical intervention is needed. It is why the Talmud, the ancient Jewish legal code offers the instruction, "One who saves even a single soul, He or She is to be viewed as if they have saved an entire world."[1] Because to that person's family, they are, in so many ways, the worth of the entire world.

Therefore, from this we affirm the fundamental right of every human being to enjoy full and unfettered access to adequate and affordable medical care and health insurance, regardless of economic circumstance.

Frank, why do you think it has been such a struggle here, in the most affluent country in the history of the world, for so many to be denied equal access to comprehensive medical care? As a physician, do you feel that every citizen of this country should have equal access to competent healthcare? Is that a right or a privilege?

Frank: It appears that when it comes to healthcare, science and religious views agree that healthcare is a right and not a privilege and I am in total agreement. Statistical evidence and theological principles all point to a right for individuals to be able to obtain medical care prevention and treatment when it is needed as well as to have it affordable. And here lies a huge problem. Healthcare in America is extremely expensive.

With an ever-increasing life expectancy and cost for healthcare, we are in dire need of finding ways to reduce healthcare costs. Drug costs alone are out of control. America is one of only two countries in the world that allows for television ads for prescription drugs (New Zealand is the other), and the saturation of daily ads to the public creates an increase in demand and usage of expensive drugs. The costs for an increasing need for operative procedures and diagnostic modalities are also extremely expensive.

One argument used by those who disagree with a universal healthcare system is that it puts into practice socialized medicine. What these individuals do not realize is that we already have in place a universal healthcare insurance plan for close to half of all Americans with Medicare, Medicaid, Military and Veteran plans.

In 1900, life expectancy was forty-seven years and when I was born in 1940 it had risen to sixty. Today that figure is close to eighty years, and it is predicted that with the advances in medicine, genetic testing, and treatment, life expectancy will reach one hundred in the not-too-distant future. With this increase will come the need for even more medical care at an ever-increasing cost. We need to do something, and we need to do it now. We need to bring the ethical principle of justice into the practice of medicine.

Mark: Frank, you have made a strong and scientific argument for a fairer healthcare system as a right that would improve the health of all Americans.

In my years as a congregational rabbi, there were congregants who came to meet with me in my office to ask for relief for their medical bills, whether for themselves or for their family members. The costs were often well beyond their reach, and they were left trying to decide which of their prescriptions they should fill. This is still true for many, despite the passage of the Affordable Care Act and the wonderful insurance of Medicare.

There were others without even basic coverage. For them, any medical care was either inaccessible or unavailable. At those times, I would reach out to the medical professionals within my congregation, asking them, imploring them, sometimes even begging them to see their fellow congregant who was seated before me. Those were difficult calls for me to make. No one should have to go begging for care in the United States of America.

That is the message I delivered from the pulpit on the High Holy Days, in the year when the Affordable Care Act was being vigorously debated in Congress. I described healthcare coverage as a fundamental human right for all, not solely for a privileged few. I based my message on a two-thousand-year-old Jewish tradition that explicitly and consistently places the preservation of human life above all else.

At the conclusion of the service, a gentleman jumped on the pulpit to tell me how strongly he disagreed with my remarks. Given the solemnity of the occasion and the dignity of the sacred space, I offered no rebuttal. That response would come, in its own way, months later, with the passage of "Obamacare," the Affordable Care Act.

We still have a long way to go to extend an equal system of medical access and care that is more just and fair. Let this be our incentive to do better, to do more for the sick among us: God has no other hands than ours to heal those who are ill, to care for and bandage the wounded, and to bring comfort to the infirm. Let us do just that.

Question for Discussion and Reflection: Do you believe universal healthcare is a right or a privilege?

NOTE

[1] Talmud, Sanhedrin, 37a.

SANCTUARY AND SAFE HARBOR

Frank: The Jewish poet, Emma Lazarus who lived from 1849 to 1887 wrote the immortal words which grace the Statue of Liberty, and which have spoken to millions of immigrants as an American message to the world, "Give me your tired, your poor, your huddled masses yearning to breathe free…"

Except for Native and African Americans, all of us are descendants of family members who left the country in which they were born and who came to the shores of America looking for a better life for themselves and their children. We are those children, and our lives are better for what they did so many years ago. We are the beneficiaries of the sacrifices they made for us to have a life of freedom and well-being. We owe them a lot.

My parents immigrated to America in 1938 to escape Nazi Germany and settled in Nashville, Tennessee, where they created a wonderful life for themselves and their family. As a young man, I often wondered how they knew that they needed to leave their home, family, and friends, as well as their business and immigrate to America. How was it that my father, who was only 30 years old when Hitler took over the government in Germany, understood that he could no longer live in the land of his ancestors and should move to a strange country?

In 1933 Germany boasted a total population of sixty-seven million citizens of which less than 1% or 523,000 were Jewish. Jews throughout Germany knew that trouble lay ahead but most hoped that the rise of national antisemitism they were seeing would eventually lessen or even abate and that life would return to some type of normalcy. Unfortunately, that did not happen.

Immigrating to America was often quite difficult during those days due to the politics of isolationism and fear. In 1917, after World War I, the United States Congress enacted the first widely restricted immigration law. It was followed by the Immigration Act of 1924 which placed quotas on the number of immigrants allowed into America from countries throughout the world. This law at that time prevented hundreds of thousands of Jews from coming to America during WWII and cost the lives of an innumerable number of innocent souls. My parents were fortunate to be able to immigrate to America.

Mark, America is experiencing a real immigration problem on our southern border today. Enormous numbers of individuals are trying to enter our country, and the American government has struggled with the ability to solve this dilemma. Does this issue seem similar to what happened to the Jewish people during the Second World War and what message can religion give to help solve this problem?

Mark: Frank, there is a plant which is called the Wandering Jew. It carries that name because, like the Jewish people throughout our history, it meanders from place to place, often without a clear path or certain trajectory.

We are nomadic people, but not by choice. Our history is one of exile and exodus from country to country, from familiar terrain to foreign land. We have fallen prey to the harshest of winds, of xenophobia, bias, and bigotry. We have learned to adapt to new circumstances and new customs, new languages, and new living conditions, often vastly different from whatever we have come to know as either familiar or predictable.

In fact, the single thing we could predict with great accuracy and reliable certainty was the temporary and tenuous nature of our existence in any place for more than a few generations at a time.

In other words, we have always been sojourners, always in the role of immigrants throughout the centuries. And much like today's immigrants, the primary motivation behind all that relocation was safety and sanctuary, the wish to gain a better life, both for us as well as for our descendants.

My parents sought refuge from the Nazi occupation of Europe, and its threat towards Jewish survival, by moving across the globe, taking refuge in Shanghai, China, one of the few places still open to Jewish escapees from Nazi oppression. I cannot imagine what they felt, leaving the European centers of art, science, and culture, to find themselves in an impoverished ghetto in a far less advanced setting in a completely foreign land as different from where they came as night is from day.

Still, despite all that, my parents met and married there. Together, they rebuilt their lives and, in 1947, were able to arrive in San Francisco as new immigrants to these Golden Shores. They knew they were the lucky ones, those Jews who had found refuge and sanctuary when so many others who tried to leave Europe could not get out in time to save their own lives. For my parents, nothing was more precious than their eligibility to secure American citizenship.

Because Jews understand the need to flee oppression, violence, and extreme poverty because of their vulnerable status, because we know the contributions immigrants can make to the countries that welcome them in, we must be strong advocates for those seeking legitimate sanctuary from harm and asylum from persecution.

An estimated 2.1 million Jews came to this country between 1880 and 1920. After 1921, those doors closed for many, and immigration rules became severely tightened and restrictive. Who knows the number of Jews who might have been saved during the Second World War had the doors been open to them? We will never know just how many lives could have been rescued from harm's way, but certainly, there would have been many. We know the painful stories of ships turned away from these shores and forced to turn back to a certain tragic fate.

The question today is in some ways the same, yet in some ways different: we need to balance our welcome to the oppressed—to "the huddled masses, yearning to be free"—with the legitimate need to secure our borders, to know who is entering this country and why they seek to enter it. Should there be a limit to the number of legal immigrants, or restrictions from certain countries or geographic areas? Frank, what do you think about this conundrum? What is the fair solution—or is there one—especially considering our own history and heritage?

Frank: Mark, you are asking some important and tough questions, and I want to try to answer them with compassion as well as doing what is right for America.

First, I am opposed to a limit on the number of legal immigrants, nor do I believe that there should exist a quota for countries or geographic areas. Country quotas prevented many German Jews from coming to America, resulting in a considerable number of deaths. These restrictions have been tried before and go against the very foundation of the American message to the world.

There is, however, a real need for America to be able to vet each immigrant to assess the appropriateness of their request to legally enter the United States. That means, our government needs to have workable guidelines on requirements for immigration and should build structures to establish secure borders to allow for orderly review of immigrant requests. Also needed is an adequate number of law enforcement personnel along with judges and administrators to manage these requests in immigration.

America must remain a beacon of hope for those who truly need and qualify for admission into our country. We have the room in America, and we have a need for immigrants to help us in fields of agriculture, construction, and a host of other work areas and professional activities.

Just as your parents and mine needed to immigrate to America, they came into the United States legally and both made significant contributions to the well-being of America. We can solve this problem if we have the will. It is the right thing to do.

Question for Discussion and Reflection: Do you believe there should be immigration quotas in America? How would you solve the problem of the overwhelming number of immigrants now facing America?

A MESSIANIC AGE

Mark: The late Elie Wiesel, noted Holocaust survivor, gifted writer, and brilliant teacher, built his legacy through the sharing of his experiences under the Nazis. He believed those lessons had eternal value in their application to other people suffering from oppression. He often ended his public appearances with a message of hope and uplift. "Jews are still waiting for the Messiah to come. Christians are waiting for the Messiah to come back again. So as long as we are both waiting, *why don't we all wait together as one?*"[1]

Traditionally, Jews professed their hopes and longings for a better day and a more peaceful world through this concept of a messiah, who would usher in a time of brotherly love and harmony, an era of peace, equality and goodwill towards all peoples, a period in which, in the words of the prophets, "They shall beat their spears into plowshares, and their swords into pruning hooks" (Isaiah 2:4).

In a similar fashion, Christians longed for the return of Jesus on earth, the second coming that might portend a similar kind of hopeful future for all those who follow his teachings.

Reform Judaism rejected this concept of a physical embodiment of a messiah. Instead, it focused its belief in striving together towards achieving a Messianic Age. The idea was, and still is, that we are God's partner in perfecting this world, in Tikkun Olam, in the repair of this broken world of ours.

Frank, as one who can look back on his eight decades of life, and who views the future through the eyes of his grandchildren, are you more hopeful or more pessimistic about their future as well as the future of all humankind? Are we closer or farther away from the arrival of a Messianic Age?

Frank: Mark, I am optimistic about the future of humankind and believe that each day brings us closer to what we Reform Jews call a Messianic Age. I am optimistic because the God I believe in has set into motion an evolutionary process that moves humans towards a caring, empathetic, loving, nonviolent state. This evolutionary process will take an exceedingly long time to come to completion, as is characteristic of evolution, however, I believe it will occur, nonetheless.

In a small way, we have already seen this process in action. Consider the state of slavery in America. Just one hundred and sixty-two years ago, President Abraham Lincoln signed the emancipation proclamation which freed four million slaves. Today the descendants of these poor and uneducated African Americans are an integral part of our society, occupying all professions and social status levels with participation on the Supreme Court, government bodies, and even president of the United States. Now that is an incredible accomplishment for the advancement of humankind in a brief period of time, moving us closer to a Messianic Age.

Consider as well that in the sixteenth century, life expectancy was twenty-nine years of age. Life was miserable for humans during those days and death came early because of diseases that could not be treated, sanitation that was not available, and an environment that was hostile in many ways. Today, life expectancy is close to eighty years of age and advances in medical treatments are truly remarkable.

These advances in the improvement of the lives of humans also occurred in a brief time and brought us closer to a Messianic Age.

Consider also that while there still exists several flash points of war around the globe, there has been a lessening of severe worldwide confrontations since the end of the Second World War in 1945. Humankind has worked arduously to have a peaceful state on earth with the establishment of the United Nations, NATO, and numerous other attempts at resolving nation conflicts. It is not perfect and far from complete, however, the evolutionary process is slowly but steadily bringing humankind to a more peaceful place.

Witness also, the ever-increasing acceptance of the LGBTQ communities around the world as another example of humankind evolving into a more accepting, inclusive society; the result of God's evolutionary process in action. This process is also in its infancy, yet over time, it will manifest itself as God's love for all humankind on earth.

A Messianic Age can be imagined for someday. The God I believe in is, by the process of survival of the fittest, effecting the behavior of all humans, moving us toward an absence of evil behavior and towards a kinder, caring, and more loving world. Examples of humans all over the world trying to repair our world are what gives me a feeling of optimism and hope.

Mark: The Jewish people could not have survived, overcome, and endured so much over the many centuries of trials and tribulations without the enduring hope of a better day. This hope is the essence of our resilience and our continued optimism in the aspirations for a brighter future, both for us and for all of humankind.

When you travel to Israel and come upon the coastline of Caesarea, the tour guides often reference a young woman who risked her life, twice, once to emigrate to pre-Israel Palestine and then again in volunteering to aid the British in their fight against the Nazis. A group of young people volunteered to parachute behind enemy lines. She was one of them. She was captured, tortured, and executed, yet never divulged the purpose of her brigade's clandestine mission.

Her name was Hannah Senesh. She sacrificed her own life to secure a better world for others whom she did not even know. Her example shows the hopeful spirit of her people and her heritage.

In her memory, the custom remains, to this day, to sing a song—a prayer if you will—reflective of her actions and her tenacious spirit, while gazing out at the Mediterranean Sea from the shores of the ancestral Jewish homeland which she called home. It is a prayer first composed by the medieval Jewish rabbi and physician, Moses Maimonides, a man of faith who was also a man of science—a prayer about his belief in the eventual coming of the Messiah. The prayer states: "Ani Ma'amin—I still believe in the coming of the Messiah, and though he may tarry, nevertheless, despite everything, I still choose to believe."[2]

May we all possess such faith. May we all believe that the arc of the universe will ultimately bend toward justice.

Question for Discussion and Reflection: How do you view a Messianic Age? How will it present itself and what will it look like?

NOTES

[1] Elie Wiesel, Memoirs: *All Rivers Run to The Sea*, (New York: Knopf, 1995), 354–355.

[2] Moses Maimonides, *The Guide for the Perplexed*, (Garden City, New York: Dover Publication, reprint 2nd ed., 1956).

EPILOGUE

As we have continued our talks and walks together, an element of holiness continues to enter the shared space between us. Together we raise new questions regarding faith and belief to find answers that comfort us. We have both often reflected on the words and ideas that comprise this book and while we feel good about what we have written, we realize there is more to think and write about as we continue our early morning walks together.

What we are doing as we walk into this metaphorical "bar" can be viewed as a sacred enterprise or sacred journey among two friends, one a man of faith and the other a man of science, both hoping to make sense and find meaning in our lives and the time we have spent on earth. It seems to us that more friends should take these walks into a "bar" or into any realm of nature or sacred space to answer the very same questions we have raised and attempted to answer, as well as others that also need asking and answering.

We have many more questions to explore and so many more of life's challenges with which to wrestle, as well as so many mysteries to unravel and understand.

We have barely touched on the issue of individual character and how that evolves, or the religious and moral expectations placed upon us by society.

We have yet to explore how we can live with integrity, honesty, generosity, and compassion in a world where those elements of character are often ignored.

What does it mean to be a "mensch," the Yiddish term for a decent and conscientious human being?

What does it mean to display the correct amount of empathy?

How do we react to the world around us that often ignores truth and facts?

How can we maintain our faith when there is so much heartache and misery around us?

How do we learn to truly listen to others and hear what is said, thereby revealing our humility, for to be humble is to listen to others even and especially when we disagree?

These and so many more questions are ones that both of us want to explore on our sacred walks together.

Despite spending a lifetime as a rabbi guiding his flock in righteous ways and a physician helping his patients traverse a path to health and motherhood, we both have become more enamored with the process of asking and then attempting to answer questions that involve the crossroads of faith, belief, religion, and science. We will do this the rest of our lives, and it is a path that others should also consider taking. Find a friend and walk into a "bar" of questioning and understanding. As we have learned, you will find peace and contentment as you walk together.

Mark and Frank

www.ingramcontent.com/pod-product-compliance
Lightning Source LLC
Chambersburg PA
CBHW070436100426
42812CB00031B/3305/J